Integrated Korean

High Intermediate 1

KLEAR Textbooks in Korean Language

Integrated Korean

High Intermediate 1

Sumi Chang

Hee-Jeong Jeong

Ho-min Sohn

Sang-Seok Yoon

University of Hawai'i Press

Honolulu

This textbook series has been developed by the Korean Language Education and Research Center (KLEAR) with the support of the Korea Foundation.

Library of Congress Cataloging-in-Publication Data

Names: Chang, Sumi, author. | Jeong, Hee-Jeong, author. | Sohn, Ho-min, author. | Yoon, Sang-Seok, author.
Title: Integrated Korean. High intermediate / Sumi Chang, Hee-Jeong Jeong, Ho-min Sohn, Sang-Seok Yoon.
Other titles: KLEAR textbooks in Korean language.
Description: Honolulu : University of Hawai'i Press, [2018] | Series: KLEAR textbooks in Korean language
Identifiers: LCCN 2018033513 | ISBN 9780824877927 (volume 1; pbk. ; alk. paper)
Subjects: LCSH: Korean language—Textbooks for foreign speakers—English.
Classification: LCC PL913 .C453 2018 | DDC 495.782/421—dc23
LC record available at https://lccn.loc.gov/2018033513

Illustrations by Seijin Han

Audio files for *High Intermediate* may be downloaded in MP3 format at https://kleartextbook.com.

Printer-ready copy has been provided by the authors.

Contents

Preface

Integrated Korean: Advanced Intermediate 1 and *2* by Ho-min Sohn and Eun-Joo Lee were published in 2003. In the last decade or so, instructors suggested revising the books to 1) update and refine the lessons, 2) introduce topics relevant to students' concerns and interests, and 3) adjust the difficulty level to allow for an easier transition from the preceding *Intermediate* volumes. These suggestions were echoed in the results of a survey conducted with a wide range of teachers who were using the *Advanced Intermediate* books.

Instead of extensively revising *Advanced Intermediate*, the present authors opted to develop an entirely new set of books entitled *High Intermediate*. They selected fourteen new lesson topics, including "Living in Korea," "Popular Korean Food," "Dating Culture in Korea," "*Hallyu*, the Korean Wave," "South Korea and North Korea," and "Korean Customs and Superstitions." Each lesson contains objectives, pre-lesson topics, conversation, activities, and readings. Corresponding information on grammar, usage, and culture is also given, and new words are listed with English glosses at the bottom of the page. Illustrations and photographs have been added to help students visualize contexts and situations.

The authors endeavored to focus equally on communication and culture learning, balancing students' development in interpersonal, interpretive, and presentational communication with helpful and interesting information on the philosophical, behavioral, and creative aspects of Korean culture. The McCune-Reischauer (M-R) Romanization System was used for Korean expressions, including linguistic examples. For proper names, the authors adopted the romanization favored by the person or the organization, which often followed the South Korean

Romanization System. When actual usage could not be verified, the M-R System was used.

The authors would like to thank all who contributed to the making of *High Intermediate*. From the early survey participants, translators, and those responsible for the visuals and audio to the many patient instructors and students involved in pilot testing the textbook drafts—their efforts helped make the final volumes possible. On behalf of KLEAR, I welcome comments and suggestions to improve the textbooks further.

Ho-min Sohn
President, KLEAR

한국의 생활 문화

Lesson 1 Living in Korea

■ 학습 목표

내용
- 자신의 의견을 이야기할 때 필요한 표현들을 배운다.
- 차이점에 대해서 이야기할 때 쓰는 표현들을 배운다.

문화
- 한국에서 생활할 때 필요한 예절과 생활 습관에 대해서 알아본다.
- 여러 나라의 문화 차이와 한국 문화의 특징에 대해 알아본다.

내용 content(s) 의견 opinion 표현 expression 차이점 difference 예절 etiquette
습관 custom; habit 특징 characteristics

■ 생각해 봅시다

가 ▸▸ 다음 질문에 대해서 서로 이야기해 봅시다.

1. 외국 사람들이 한국에서 생활할 때 어떤 점들이 불편할까요?

2. 한국의 예절에 대해서 얼마나 알고 있습니까?
   한국의 여러 가지 예절에 대해서 아는 것들을 이야기해 봅시다.

3. 한국 친구에게 한국에서 생활할 때 주의해야 할 점들에 대해서
   물어보고 같이 이야기해 봅시다.

4. 외국 사람들이 여러분 나라에서 생활할 때 알아 두어야 할
   예절들은 뭐가 있을까요?

나 ▸▸ 다음 중에서 여러분 문화에서 실례가 되는 질문은 어떤 것들이
   있을까요?

1. 나이가 어떻게 되세요? 몇 년생이세요?

2. 교회 다니세요? 종교가 어떻게 되세요?

-점 thing, point 여러 가지 various, many 주의하다 to be cautious, careful 알아 두다 to keep in mind 실례 discourtesy ~년생 ~ year born 종교 religion

3. 무슨 일을 하세요? 월급은 얼마나 받으세요?

4. 아버지가 어떤 일을 하세요?

5. 어느 대학에 다니세요? 어느 대학을 졸업하셨어요?

6. 남자/여자 친구가 있으세요?

7. 결혼하셨어요? 언제 결혼할 거예요? 왜 아직 결혼을 안 하셨어요?

8. 아이는 있으세요? 몇 명이에요? 왜 아이를 안 낳으세요?

9. 어느 정당을 지지하세요?

10. 키가 얼마나 되세요? 체중이 얼마나 되세요?

다 ▸ 위 질문들 이외에 여러분 나라에서 물어보면 실례가 되는 질문이
있습니까? 이야기해 봅시다.

월급 salary 아이를 낳다 to give birth to a baby 정당 political party 지지하다 to support
체중 body weight 이외 besides, except

한국 생활

한국어 연수 프로그램에 갔다 온 후 한국어 수업에서

선생님: 여러분들 한국 생활 재미있었어요? 한국에 있는 동안 한국**에 대해서**[GU1.1] 느꼈던 점들을 좀 얘기해 주세요.

제니: 한국 대학에는 대부분 한국 학생들만 다녀서 그게 좀 신기했어요. 미국 대학에는 여러 인종들이 있고 유학생들도 많잖아요.

노아: 맞아요. 그래서 가끔 제가 눈에 띄어서 좀 불편할 때도 있었어요.

선생님: 그랬겠네요. 혹시 한국 친구들과 지내면서 문화 차이 때문에 당황했던 적이 있으면 이야기해 주세요.

노아: 저는 한국 친구들이 저한테 머리가 작다, 얼굴이 작다고 해서 처음엔 무슨 말인지 몰랐어요.

선생님: 그거 칭찬인데요.

노아: 네, 이제는 알아요. 근데 저는 얼굴이나 머리가 작다, 크다, 이런 말을 한국에서 처음 들었거든요. 저는 머리가 나쁘다는 뜻인 줄 알고 처음에는 좀 기분이 나빴어요.

연수 (educational) training ~에 대해서 about 느끼다 to feel 대부분 mostly 신기하다 to be surprising, novel 인종 race, ethnic group 눈에 띄다 to stand out, to attract attention 혹시 by any chance 당황하다 to be flustered 처음엔 = 처음에는 at first 칭찬 compliment 이제 now 뜻 meaning 기분 feeling

제니: 저도 그런 얘기를 들은 적이 있어요. 제 **생각에는**^{GU1.2} 한국 사람들이 미국 사람들**에 비해서**^{GU1.3} 외모에 관심이 더 많은 것 같아요. 한국 학생들은 보통 학교에 올 때에도 옷을 잘 입고 오더라고요. 미국 학생들 중에도 옷을 잘 입는 학생들이 있지만 보통은 신경을 잘 안 쓰거든요. 저도 그렇고…

선생님: 제니 씨는 옷을 잘 입던데요.

제니: 아니에요. 저는 옷 잘 못 입어요. 근데 한국에 갔다 온 후에는 좀 더 신경을 쓰고 있어요.

선생님: 그렇군요. 또 다른 것들은 뭐가 있었나요?

린다: 저는 한국에서 나이를 따지는 것이 이상했어요. 미국에서는 나이가 그냥 **법적인**^{GU1.4} 개념이거든요. 제가 살던 곳에서는 16살이 되면 운전면허를 딸 수 있고, 18살 때 투표권을 얻고, 21살 때부터 술을 마실 수 있고… 그런데 보통 친구 사이에는 나이를 크게 신경 안 써요.

선생님: 그럼 친구들이 나이를 물어봐서 기분 나빴던 적이 있었어요?

린다: 저는 괜찮지만 나이를 물어보는 것은 좀 사적인 질문이니까 기분 나빠하는 사람도 있을 거예요.

제니: 그렇지만 한국에서는 자기보다 나이가 많으면 존댓말을 해야 하니까 나이를 물어보는 거라고 들었어요. 근데 저는 나이를 어떻게 물어보는 것이 좋은지 잘 모르겠어요. 그냥 "몇 살이에요?"라고 하면 좀 실례지요?

~에 비해서 compare to ~ 외모 appearance 관심 interest 신경을 쓰다 to pay attention to, to care 따지다 to argue over (a small matter) 법적이다 to be legal 개념 concept 운전면허 driver's license 따다 to get, obtain 투표권 right to vote 사적이다 to be personal 존댓말 honorific language

선생님: 그렇죠. 나이를 알아내는 것은 한국 사람들한테도 쉽지 않아
요. **어떤**^{GU1.5} 사람들은 "몇 년생이에요?"라고 태어난 해를 물
어보기도 하고 "몇 학번이에요?"라고 언제 대학에 입학했는
지 물어보기도 해요. 그런데 나이가 적은 사람이라도 아직 친
하지 않으면 존댓말을 쓰는 것이 좋아요. 친해지면 자연스럽
게 반말을 쓸 수 있어요.

노아: 아, 나이**뿐만 아니라**^{GU1.6} 얼마나 친한지도 중요하네요. 한국
사람들과 대화를 잘 하**기 위해서는**^{GU1.7} 문화를 잘 알아야 하는
것 같아요.

선생님: 물론이지요. 여러분들이 한국어를 더 잘 하기 위해서는 한국
문화에 대해서 많이 알아야 하니까 계속 관심을 가져 보세요.

알아내다 to find out, figure out 해 year 학번 the year when one enters a college 입학하다
to enter a school 친하다 to be close 자연스럽게 naturally 반말 non-honorific language
물론이지요. Of course. 관심을 가지다 to have interests

이해 문제

가... 다음 내용이 대화의 내용과 같으면 ○, 다르면 X에 표시하세요.

1. 한국 대학에는 많은 외국 학생들이 다닌다.   ○   X

2. 한국 사람들한테 머리가 작다고 하면 실례가 될 수 있다.   ○   X

3. 미국 사람들은 한국 사람들보다 외모에 관심이 많은 것 같다.   ○   X

4. 미국 사람들은 보통 나이에 대해서 별로 신경을 안 쓴다.   ○   X

5. 한국에서는 나이가 어린 사람에게는 편하게 반말을 쓸 수 있다.   ○   X

나... 다음 질문에 대답해 보세요.

1. 위 대화에 나온 한국과 미국의 문화 차이를 정리해 봅시다.

2. 위 대화의 내용 중 여러분이 제일 이해하기 어려운 한국 문화는 어떤 것입니까?

3. 존댓말과 반말을 바르게 쓰기 위해서는 어떤 점들을 생각해야 합니까?

문법과 용법

GU1.1

~에 대해(서) 'about, in regard to'

저는 한국 사회에 **대해(서)** 더 배우고 싶어요.

I want to learn more about Korean society.

요즘 한국 드라마에 **대한** 사람들의 관심이 높아지고 있다.

People's interest in Korean dramas is increasing these days.

▶ This pattern expresses the concept 'about (something or someone)'. It is derived from the combination of the particle 에 'to/in/at', the verb 대하다 'face, confront', and the connective ending –여(서) 'by, so, and then'. ~에 대해(서) is a contraction of ~에 대하여(서), which is used in formal speech and written style. The modifier form is ~에 대한 'about', which consists of 에 대하– and the modifier ending ~ㄴ.

▶ A synonymous pattern is ~에 관해(서), 'regarding, concerning, about, with regard to', which is derived from the combination of ~에, the verb 관하다 'refer to, be about', and the connective ending –여(서). ~에 관해(서) is a contraction of ~에 관하여(서), which is used in formal speech and written style. Its modifier form is ~에 관한.

GU1.2

X 생각에(는) 'in X's opinion'

제 **생각에** 그 영화는 별로였어요.

In my opinion, that movie was not very good.

네 **생각에는** 언제까지 숙제를 다 할 수 있을 것 같아?

In your opinion, when does it seem like you can finish the homework?

▶ This pattern requires X to be a human noun or pronoun and 생각 'thinking, idea, opinion, conception' to be followed by the particle 에 'to/in/at'. The particle 은/는 may be added if emphasis or contrast of X 생각에 is called for. The particle 에 in 에(는) can be replaced by the particle 으로 'with', as in 토니 생각에(는) and 토니 생각으로(는) 'in Tony's opinion'.

GU1.3

~에 비해(서) 'compared to'

작년**에 비해(서)** 올해 여름이 더 더운 것 같다.

Compared to last year, this summer seems to be hotter.

한국 사람들이 미국 사람들**에 비해(서)** 신용카드를 더 많이 쓰는 편이다.

Compared to Americans, Koreans tend to use credit cards more often.

▶ This pattern expresses comparison. It is composed of the particle 에 followed by the verb 비하다 'compare' and the connective ending –여(서) 'by, so, and then'.

~에 비해(서) is a contraction of ~에 비하여(서), which is used in formal speech and written style.

▶ Comparison is also expressed by ~에 비하면 'if/when compared to', as in 서울에 비하면 제주도는 춥지 않아요, '(if/when) compared to Seoul, Jeju Island is not cold'.

~적 '–ic, –ical'

저는 경제**적(인)** 이유로 학교를 그만두었습니다.

I quit school for financial reasons.

제주도는 세계**적**으로 유명한 관광지입니다.

Jeju Island is a world-famous tourist attraction.

▶ The Sino-Korean suffix –적 changes a Sino-Korean noun to an adjective-like word, as in 경제 'economy' to 경제적 'economic'; 민주 'democracy' to 민주적 'democratic'; 정치 'politics' to 정치적 'political'; 개인 'private person' to 개인적 'personal'; 감동 'impression' to 감동적 'impressive'; and 법 'law' to 법적 'legal'. In Korean, these adjective-like words are treated as "adjectival" nouns. In order to be used as adjectives, they are followed by the copula 이 'be' or 아니 'be not', as in 그 영화는 감동적이었어요 'That movie was impressive' and 비싼 물건을 사는 것은 경제적이 아니에요 'It is uneconomical to buy expensive things'. The modifier form is –적(인), as in 경제적 문제 or 경제적인 문제 'economic problem'.

▶ The adverbial form is –적으로 '-ly, -ically', as in 미국은 경제적으로나 군사적으로나 세계에서 가장 강한 나라다 'The United States is the strongest nation in the world, both economically and militarily'.

GU1.5

어떤 'certain, some, some kind of'

저 배우를 **어떤** 드라마에서 봤는데 이름은 모르겠어요.

I saw that actor in some drama, but I don't know his name.

어떤 사람이 전화를 했어요.

Someone called you.

▶ All Korean question words are used as indefinite words as well, as in 무엇 'what, something', 누구 'who, someone', 어디 'where, some place', 언제 'when, sometime', 어떻게 'how, in some way', 왜 'why, for some reason'. Similarly, the pre-noun question word 어떤 (derived from 어떠한) 'which, what kind of' is also used as an indefinite word in the sense of 'some, certain, some kind of'. For example, 어떤 옷을 샀니? has two meanings: 'What kind of clothes did you buy?' [with falling intonation] and 'Did you buy some kind of clothes?' [with rising intonation].

GU1.6

~뿐(만) 아니라 'not only ... but also ...'

린다는 한국어**뿐만 아니라** 일본어도 할 수 있어요.

Not only can Linda speak Korean, she can also speak Japanese.

저는 소주**뿐 아니라** 맥주도 안 마셔요.

Not only do I not drink soju, I also do not drink beer.

오늘은 바람이 많이 불 **뿐만 아니라** 아주 춥다.

It is not only windy, but also very cold today.

▶ This pattern expresses that two parallel states or events are equally positive or equally negative. It consists of the bound noun/particle 뿐 'only, alone, just, nothing but', followed optionally by the "emphasis" particle 만 'only', and the negative copula connective 아니라 (아니 'be not' + 라 'and/but'), to mean 'not just … but'. This pattern is followed by a second clause to mean '… as well'.

▶ 뿐 is a bound noun, in that it is always preceded either by a noun/pronoun or a verb/adjective. A noun/pronoun is directly placed before –뿐, as in 내가 사랑하는 사람은 너뿐이야 'It is only you that I love'. A verb/adjective is placed before 뿐 only in the modifier form with the prospective ending –(으)ㄹ, as in 미아는 하루 종일 울 뿐이다 'Mia does nothing but cry all day long'.

GU1.7

~기 위해(서)   'in order to, so as to, for the purpose of'

나는 더 건강해지**기 위해(서)** 매일 운동을 해요.
I exercise every day in order to get healthier.

한국어를 잘 하**기 위해서**는 매일 연습해야 돼요.
In order to speak Korean well, you have to practice every day.

▶ This pattern indicates that the following action is carried out with a goal or purpose of achieving the preceding action. It is composed of the "nominalizer" suffix –기 followed by the verb 위하다 'to serve, devote oneself' and the connective ending –여(서). ~기 위해(서) is a contraction of the more formal ~기 위하여(서). The pre-noun modifier form is ~기 위한 'for the sake of', as in 건강을 위한 노력 'efforts for (one's) health'.

▶ Instead of a verb/adjective + –기, a noun or pronoun + object particle 을/를 can be placed before 위해(서), as in 나라를 위하여 'for the country' and 건강을 위해 (서) 'for (one's) health'.

활동

가... 보기의 표현을 사용하여 다음 영어 문장에 맞게 빈 칸을 채워 보세요.

> ~에 비해서, 제 생각에는, ~(으)ㄹ 뿐만 아니라, ~기 위해, 어떤 ~

1. In my opinion, that movie was not very good.

   _____ 저 영화는 별로였어요.

2. Compared to last year, this summer is hotter.

   _____ 이번 여름이 더 더워요.

3. Someone called you.

   _____ 전화했어요.

4. It is not only windy, but also very cold today.

   오늘은 _____ 아주 추워요.

5. In order to speak Korean better, you have to practice every day.

   _____ 매일 연습해야 돼요.

나... 빈 칸에 가장 알맞은 말을 고르세요.

1. 빨간색 옷을 입으면 눈에 잘 _____ .

   ㄱ. 띄어요   ㄴ. 봐요   ㄷ. 맞아요   ㄹ. 뵈어요

2. 저한테 신경 _____ 마세요. 제가 혼자 갈 수 있어요.

    ㄱ. 하지   ㄴ. 쓰지   ㄷ. 내지   ㄹ. 보이지

3. 저는 이번 여름에 운전 면허를 꼭 _____ .

    ㄱ. 딸 거예요   ㄴ. 이길 거예요   ㄷ. 만들 거예요   ㄹ. 생길 거예요

4. 저는 한국 역사에 많은 관심을 _____ 있어요.

    ㄱ. 보고   ㄴ. 들고   ㄷ. 가지고   ㄹ. 듣고

5. 윗사람한테는 특히 예절을 잘 _____ 됩니다.

    ㄱ. 해야   ㄴ. 보여야   ㄷ. 드려야   ㄹ. 지켜야

다... 한국에서는 어떤 사람을 보통 예쁘다거나 잘생겼다고 하는지 한국 사람들에게
    물어보고 정리해서 발표해 봅시다.

라... 여러분 나라의 사람들은 나이에 대해서 어떻게 생각합니까?
    사람을 만날 때 나이는 얼마나 중요합니까?

마... 여러분은 외국에서 살거나 다른 나라 사람들과 생활하면서 문화 차이 때문에
    당황했던 적이 있습니까? 문화 차이 때문에 있었던 일들에 대해서 이야기해 봅시다.

읽기

한국에 가세요?

"로마에 가면 로마 법을 따르라"라는 말이 있는 것처럼 한국에 가서는 한국의 예절과 생활 습관을 잘 지키는 것이 중요하다. 특히 한국에서는 자기보다 나이가 많거나 사회적 지위가 높은 사람을 대하는 것과 그렇지 않은 사람을 대하는 것이 다르다. 따라서, 윗사람에 대한 예절에 특히 신경을 써야 한다. **예를 들어,**^{GU1.8} 가까운 친구들에게는 보통 손을 흔들면서 인사를 하면 되지만 선생님에게는 반드시 고개를 숙여 인사를 해야 한다.

악수를 할 때에도 아랫사람이 두 손으로 윗사람의 손을 잡고 고개를 숙이면서 하는 것을 볼 수 있다. 악수는 원래 서양**식**^{GU1.9} 인사법이지만 한국에서는 한국**식** 악수 방법이 있는 것이다. 그리고 아랫사람이 윗사람에게 물건을 드리거나 받을 때에, 술이나 물을 따르거나 받을 때에도 두 손을 사용해야 한다. 개인적으로 윗사람에게 돈을 드릴 일이 있으면 돈을 봉투에 넣어서 드리는 것이 좋다.

한국에서 학교에 다닌다면 수업 예절을 알아 **둘**^{GU1.10} **필요가 있다.**^{GU1.11} 수업 중에 모자를 쓰거나 노출이 많은 옷을 입으면 예의에

따르다 to follow ‑처럼 like, as if 특히 especially 자기 oneself 사회적 지위 social status 대하다 to deal with, treat 따라서 accordingly, therefore 윗사람 someone of older or higher status 예를 들어 for example 손을 흔들다 to wave (one's) hand(s) 반드시 = 꼭 for sure; must 고개를 숙이다 to bow 악수 shaking hands 원래 originally 서양식 the Western style 따르다 to pour 개인적 personal 노출 exposure 예의에 어긋나다 to go against manners

어긋난다고 생각될 수 있다. 의자에 앉을 때 너무 뒤로 기대거나 똑바로 앉지 않으면 수업에 열심히 집중하지 않고 있다고 생각될 수 있으니 주의해야 한다. 그리고 수업 중에 껌을 씹거나 음식을 먹는 것도 바람직하지 않다. 선생님께 질문을 할 때에는 선생님이 말하는 중간에 끼어드는 것은 좋지 않으며^{GU1.12} 선생님이 질문을 하라고 할 때에 손을 들고 질문을 한다.

　한국 사람의 집을 방문할 때에도 주의해야 할 점들이^{GU1.13} 있다. 집 안에서는 보통 신발을 신지 않는데, 집에 들어가서 신발을 벗어 놓는 곳을 현관이라고 한다. 또한 식사를 할 때에는 제일 나이가 많은 사람이 식사를 시작하실 때까지 기다려야 한다. 그리고 다른 사람들보다 빨리 식사를 끝냈을 때에도 모두 식사가 끝날 때까지 기다린다. 식사를 시작하기 전에는 "잘 먹겠습니다", 식사를 끝낸 후에는 "잘 먹었습니다"라고 인사를 하면 좋다.

　다른 나라에서 생활할 때 그 나라의 생활 습관을 잘 아는 것이 물론 중요하지만 더 중요한 것은 새로운 문화를 존중하고 배우려고 노력하는 자세이다.

기대다 to lean on 똑바로 straight, upright 집중하다 to concentrate –으니 formal form of –으니까 껌 chewing gum 씹다 to chew 바람직하다 to be desirable 끼어들다 to cut in 손을 들다 to raise one's hand(s) 방문하다 to visit 또한 also 끝내다 to finish (something) 끝나다 to be over, done 존중하다 to respect 자세 attitude

이해 문제

가... 다음 내용이 본문의 내용과 같으면 ○, 다르면 X에 표시하세요.

1. 한국에서는 윗사람한테 하는 인사법과
   아랫사람에게 하는 인사법이 다르다   ○   X

2. 윗사람은 아랫사람에게 두 손으로 물건을 주거나 받아야 한다.   ○   X

3. 한국에서는 수업에 갈 때 노출이 심한 옷은 피한다.   ○   X

4. 한국 사람들은 집 안에서 신발을 신지 않는다.   ○   X

5. 한국에서 식사할 때에는 윗사람들보다 빨리 먹는 것이 좋다.   ○   X

나... 다음 질문에 대답해 보세요.

1. 윗 글에서 "나이가 많거나 사회적 지위가 높은 사람"을 뜻하는 말을 찾아서
   써 보세요.

2. 한국 사람들은 윗사람과 악수를 할 때 보통 어떻게 합니까?

3. 한국에서 수업 시간에 하면 좋지 않은 것들을 모두 찾아서 써 보세요.

4. "현관"은 어떤 곳입니까?

5. 한국에서 식사할 때 주의해야 할 점은 어떤 것이 있습니까?

문법과 용법

예를 들어(서)/들면 'for example'

한국과 미국의 문화 차이에 대해 **예를 들어(서)** 설명해 주세요.

Please explain the cultural differences between Korea and the U.S.,
using examples.

많은 한국 음식은 발효 음식이다. **예를 들면**, 김치, 된장, 간장은
매일 먹는 발효 음식이다.

Many Korean foods are fermented. For example, kimchi, bean paste,
and soy sauce are fermented foods that are eaten every day.

▶ The Sino-Korean noun 예 'example, case, instance' compounds with the object
particle and the transitive verb 들다 'raise, hold up' to mean 'to present an
example' or 'for example'. With the ending ~어(서) 'by, so, and then', it means
'by presenting an example', while with the "conditional" ending ~면 'if', it
means 'for example'.

~식 'way, style'

짜장면은 한국**식** 중국 음식이에요.
Jjajangmyon is a Korean style Chinese food.

이런 **식**으로 공부하면 금방 한국어를 잘 말하게 될 거예요.

If you study in this way, you will speak Korean well in no time.

▶ The Sino-Korean noun 식 'ceremony, formula, method, style, mode, way, manner' is used as a nominal suffix as well, especially after a Sino-Korean noun, as in 한국식 'Korean style', 미국식 'American style', 중국식 'Chinese style', 현대식 'modern style', and 구식 'old style'. Examples of its common use as a noun include 나는 내 식으로 살래요 'I am going to live how I want to' and 그런 식으로 써서는 안 돼 'Don't write it that way'.

GU1.10

~어/아 두다/놓다
'do something for future use/reference'

손님이 많이 올 것 같아서 음식을 많이 **해 두**었어요.

I prepared a lot of food because it seemed there would be many guests.

다음 주에 시험이 있으니 주말에 공부를 많이 **해 놓**으세요.

Since you have a test next week, make sure to study enough over the week-end.

▶ The verbs 두다 and 놓다 mean 'put, place, deposit, leave aside'. When used as an auxiliary verb as in ~어/아 두다/놓다, 두다 or 놓다 indicates that the action is performed for future use or advantage. Thus, for example, 창문을 열어 두었어요 'I left the windows open' implies 'for future use, e.g., to let cool air come in'.

GU1.11

~(으)ㄹ 필요가 있다/없다
'It is necessary/unnecessary to'

건강을 유지하려면 운동을 꾸준히 할 **필요가 있다**.

If you want to maintain your health, it is necessary to exercise constantly.

이 숙제는 길게 쓸 **필요가 없어요**. 한 쪽만 쓰면 돼요.

You don't need to write a lot for this homework. It would be fine to write only
1 page.

▶ The noun 필요 means 'necessity, need, requirement'. Its verb form is 필요하다
'be necessary, needed, required', as in 돈이 필요하다 'I need money'. In order
to indicate 'it is necessary/unnecessary to do something', the pattern ~(으)ㄹ
필요가 있다/없다, which is composed of the prospective modifier ending ~(으)
ㄹ followed by 필요, the subject particle, and the existential adjective 있다/없다.
Literally, it means 'the need to do something exists/does not exist'.

GU1.12

~(으)며 'and'

오늘은 흐리**며** 바람이 불겠습니다.

It will be cloudy and windy today.

오늘 파티에 몇 명이 왔**으며** 누가 왔는지 알려 주세요.

Please let me know how many people and who came to today's party.

▶ The "addition" connective ending ~(으)며 is a formal counterpart of ~고 'and'. Compared to ~고, ~(으)며 is more often used in formal situations or in writing. Both ~(으)며 and ~고 may be preceded by tense markers, as in 오늘은 흐리며/흐리고; 어제는 흐렸으며/흐렸고; and 내일은 흐리겠으며/흐리겠고.

GU1.13

~ 점   'point, spot, dot, aspect, ...'

모든 사람들에게는 배울 **점**이 있다.

Eveyone has something (some points) to learn.

도시에 살면 좋은 **점**과 나쁜 **점**이 있다.

Living in a city has both positive (good points) and negative (bad points) aspects.

▶ The Sino-Korean noun 점 'point, spot, dot, mark, score, piece, aspect, respect' is used either as an independent noun or as a part of a compound. The above example sentences illustrate independent uses. Some more examples are 점을 찍다 'mark with a dot' and 이 점에 대해서는 할 말이 없다 'I have nothing to say in this respect'. Uses of a part of compounds include 장점 '(one's) strong points, merits', 단점 'shortcomings, drawback', 출발점 'starting point', and 공통점 'common points'.

활동

■■
■■

가... 밑줄 친 단어와 <u>반대의 뜻</u>을 가진 단어를 고르세요.

1. 선생님과 이야기를 할 때에는 <u>존댓말</u>을 써야 해요.

ㄱ.반말   ㄴ.바른말   ㄷ.나쁜 말   ㄹ.높임말

2. 악수는 원래 <u>서양</u>식 인사예요

ㄱ.유럽   ㄴ.동양   ㄷ.동쪽   ㄹ.남쪽

3. <u>짝수</u> 날에는 이쪽에 주차하세요.

ㄱ.번호   ㄴ.횟수   ㄷ.홀수   ㄹ.지위

4. 꿈에 돼지를 보면 <u>행운</u>이 찾아온대요.

ㄱ.행복   ㄴ.불운   ㄷ.다행   ㄹ.운세

5. 집에 들어갈 때에는 현관에서 신발을 <u>벗으세요.</u>

ㄱ.입으세요   ㄴ.신으세요   ㄷ.하세요   ㄹ.쓰세요

나... 보기의 표현을 사용해서 다음 영어 문장의 의미에 맞게 빈 칸을 채우세요.

~식, 예를 들면, ~(으)며, ~(으)ㄹ 필요가 있다, ~점

---

1. Prof. Kim is a medical doctor as well as a poet.

김 교수님은 _____ 시인이십니다.

2. For example, kimchi is a famous fermented food.

_____ 김치는 유명한 발효 음식이에요.

3. *Jjajangmyeon* is a Korean style Chinese food.

짜장면은 _____ 중국 음식이에요.

4. I need to prepare a lot of food for tomorrow's party.

저는 내일 파티를 위해 음식을 많이 _____.

5. Everyone has something to learn.

모든 사람들은 _____이 있다.

다... 한국의 인사법과 여러분 나라의 인사법의 차이에 대해서 이야기해 봅시다.

라... 한국과 여러분 나라의 학교 생활에서 볼 수 있는 문화적 차이에 대해서
     이야기해 봅시다.

마... 여러분 나라의 식사 예절에 대해서 짧은 글을 써 봅시다.

바... 여러분은 다음 상황에서 어떻게 행동하시겠습니까?

    1. 저녁 식사에 초대받아 충분히 먹었는데 친구 어머니가 자꾸 더 먹으라고 할 때

    2. 술을 못 마시는데 회식에서 직장 상사/선배가 술을 권할 때

    3. 수업 중에 화장실에 가고 싶을 때

    4. 친구가 머리 모양을 바꿨는데 전혀 안 어울릴 때

    5. 친구가 내 컴퓨터를 빌려 달라고 할 때

사... 다음 사진을 보고 한국의 술자리 예절과 여러분 나라의 술자리 예절의 차이점에 대해서 이야기해 봅시다.

아... 여러분 문화와 한국 문화의 비슷한 점과 다른 점에 대해서 글을 써 봅시다.
    글을 쓸 때 "제 생각에는…" "~에 비해서" "예를 들어서" "~ 점"
    "~에 대해서"와 같은 표현들을 써 봅시다.

술자리 drinking party 모임 gathering 연말 end of the year 어른 (one's) elders; adult 이용
use 예의상 out of courtesy 적당히 moderately 취기 the effects of alcohol 실수 mistake

추가 읽기

재미있는 숫자 이야기

숫자에 담긴 의미는 각 문화마다 다른데 한국에도 좋게 생각되는 숫자들과 나쁘게 생각되는 숫자들이 있다. 먼저 좋은 숫자로는 1, 3, 7, 10이 있다. 1은 첫 번째, 1위, 1등급 등 최고를 표현할 때 쓰이므로 많은 사람들이 좋아한다. 그리고 '인생에는 3번의 기회가 찾아온다', '삼세판' 등 3도 좋은 숫자로 생각된다. 그리고 서양에서와 마찬가지로 한국에서도 7은 행운의 숫자로 사람들이 좋아하는 숫자이다. 예를 들어 일주일은 7일이며 무지개의 색깔을 일곱 가지로 나눈다. 한국에서는 결혼식에 갈 때 보통 돈을 선물하는데, 3만 원, 5만 원 등 10만 원 미만은 홀수로 주는 것이 보통이고 2만 원, 4만 원, 6만 원, 8만 원 등 짝수로는 주지 않는다. 하지만 10만 원은 괜찮다. 10은 모든 계산의 기본이 되는 숫자이고 '완성'을 상징하기 때문이다.

안 좋은 숫자로는 4와 9가 있다. 4는 한자 죽을 사(死)와 발음이 같아서 좋지 않은 숫자로 생각했다. 그래서 건물 4층을 'F'로 표시하기도 한다. 그리고 한국에서는 19살, 29살, 39살처럼 9로 끝나는 나이를 '아홉수'라고 부르며 나쁜 일이 생기기 쉬운 나이라고 생각한다. 아마도 완성의 숫자인 10을 앞두고 몸과 마음을 조심하라는 뜻이 담겨 있는 것으로 생각된다.

담기다 to be contained   숫자 number   의미 meaning   각~마다 for each ~   ~로는 as ~
1등급 top-grade   최고 the best   표현하다 to express   쓰이다 to be used   인생 (one's) life
기회 chance   삼세판 the best of three   마찬가지로 similarly   무지개 rainbow   홀수 odd
number   짝수 even number   계산 calculation   완성 completion   상징하다 to symbolize
표시하다 to mark, indicate

한국에서 자주 쓰는 서양 속담

- 로마에 가면 로마법을 따르라. When in Rome, do as the Romans do.

- 일찍 일어나는 새가 벌레를 잡는다. The early bird catches the worm.

- 뜻이 있는 곳에 길이 있다. Where there is a will, there is a way.

- 시간이 금이다. Time is gold.

- 그 아버지의 그 아들. Like father, like son.

- 하늘은 스스로 돕는 자를 돕는다.

    Heaven helps those who help themselves.

- 아는 것이 힘이다. Knowledge is power.

- 피는 물보다 진하다. Blood is thicker than water.

- 무소식이 희소식이다. No news is good news.

- 구르는 돌에는 이끼가 끼지 않는다. A rolling stone gathers no moss.

- 연습이 완벽을 만든다. Practice makes perfect.

- 필요는 발명의 어머니. Necessity is the mother of invention.

▖▚ 번역문 ▖▚

CONVERSATION: Life in Korea

After a Korean language training program

Teacher: Class, did you enjoy living in Korea? Please share about some of the things you felt during your time in Korea.

Jenny: In Korean colleges, there are mainly just Korean students, and that was pretty interesting. U.S. colleges have a variety of different ethnic groups and a lot of exchange students.

Noah: Right. So sometimes I felt uncomfortable because I stood out (so much).

Teacher: Ah, I bet it was like that. By any chance, was there ever a time when you were taken aback by a culture difference with your Korean friends? Please share about that.

Noah: At first when my Korean friends would tell me that I have a small head or a small face I didn't know what it meant.

Teacher: That's a compliment.

Noah: Yes, now I know. But Korea is the first place that I've heard someone talk about a head or face being big or small. At first, I thought it meant I wasn't smart, so it put me in a bad mood.

Jenny: I've heard the same thing. I think that Korean people seem to be more interested in physical appearances than Americans are. Based on my experience, Korean students dress well even when at school. In the U.S., there are students who dress well too, but you know, people usually don't care that much. I'm the same way…

Teacher: But you dress well too, you know.

Jenny: No, I don't dress well. But after having gone to Korea I now pay more attention to how I dress.

Teacher: I see. What other aspects of Korean culture were hard to understand?

Linda: I thought it was a little strange how big of a deal age is in Korea. In the U.S. age is just a legal concept. For example, where I lived, you can get a driver's license when you turn 16, you get the right to vote at 18, and starting when you're 21 you can drink alcohol. But in personal relationships people don't care that much about age.

Teacher: So, was there ever a time when someone asked your age and it put you in a bad mood?

Linda: I was fine with it, but I think that asking a person's age is kind of a personal question, so there are people who would be put off by it.

Jenny: I heard though that in Korea, people ask each other's ages because if someone is older than you, then you need to use the honorific form. But I don't know what a good way to ask someone's age would be. Just saying "How old are you?" would be a little rude right?

Teacher: That's right. Finding out a person's age isn't easy for Korean people either. Some people ask "What year are you?" to ask what year someone was born in, and some people ask "What's your college entrance number?" in order to ask what year someone started college. However, if you're not close to someone yet it's a good idea to use the honorific form even if they're younger than you. If you become close you can naturally use informal speech with them.

Noah: Ah, so it's not just age, but also how close you are that's important. It seems like in order to have a good conversation with Korean people there are a lot of cultural things you need to know.

Teacher: Of course. In order to speak Korean well you all need to understand a lot about Korean culture, so please try to maintain your interest in it.

READING: You're Going to Korea?

Like the saying "When in Rome, do as the Romans do", when going to Korea it is important to observe Korean etiquette and lifestyle practices. In Korea, one treats a person who is older or of a higher social status different than someone who is not, and so it is especially important to pay attention to etiquette as it relates to one's elders. For example, while it's okay to wave to close friends as you greet them, when you greet a teacher you must bow your head.

One will also see that when shaking hands the person of a lower status will grasp the elder's hand with both hands while lowering their head. While the handshake is originally a Western method of greeting, in Korea, there is a Korean method of shaking hands. Additionally, when a person of lower status gives to or receives something from an elder, or when they pour or accept alcohol or water, they must use two hands. If a person of lower status is personally giving an elder money, it is a good idea to put the money in an envelope.

If you are attending school in Korea, you need to understand classroom etiquette. It is considered impolite to wear a hat or wear clothing that is very revealing in class. Since leaning back too far in your chair or not sitting properly will lead people to think you're not focusing well in class, you need to be careful. It is also recommended not to chew gum or eat during class. When asking the teacher a question, it is not a good idea to interrupt the teacher, and when the teacher asks for questions, you should raise your hand and then ask your question.

There are also things to be aware of when visiting a Korean person's house. In Korea, people usually do not wear shoes indoors. Therefore, before you enter a house in Korea, you need to take your shoes off. The place in front of a door where you can leave your shoes is called a *hyŏn'gwan*. Also, when having a meal, you should wait until the oldest person at the table starts eating first. Additionally, even if you finish eating before everyone else, you should remain seated and wait until everyone has finished. It is also good to say "I will eat well", before eating, and "I ate well" after one has finished their meal.

When you are in a different country it is, of course, important to know about that country's lifestyle practices, but it is more important to respect the new culture and to have an attitude of trying to learn about the new culture.

FURTHER READING: Fun Facts about Numbers

Numbers have different meanings in every culture, and in Korea too, there are numbers thought to be good and other numbers thought to be bad. First, the good numbers include 1, 3, 7, 10. Lots of people like the number 1 because it is used to express the best things, as in "first", "first place", and "first class". The number 3 is also thought of as being a good number considering there are many phrases with 3 in them such as "best out of three" and "In life there are three opportunities". Also, just as in the West, in Korea the number 7 is well liked because it is thought of as being a lucky number. For example, in a week there are seven days, and a rainbow is divided up into seven colors. At weddings in Korea people usually give money as a gift, and when giving less than 100,000 won it is normal to give an amount in which the first number is odd, such as 30,000, or 50,000 won, etc.... Gifts are not given in amounts where the first number is even such as 20,000, 40,000, 60,000, or 80,000 won. However, giving 100,000 won is acceptable. This is because the number 10 is the foundation of all calculations and symbolizes "completion".

4 and 9 are examples of bad numbers. The number 4 is pronounced the same way as the Chinese character for death, and as such, is thought of as being a bad number. Therefore, the fourth floor in buildings is sometimes labeled as "F". Also, in Korea, ages like 19, 29, and 39 that have the number 9 in them are called "ahopsu", and it is thought that bad things can easily happen at these ages. Perhaps this is thought because one should be careful with their heart and mind considering 9 comes right before 10, the number of completion.

■■ 단어 ■■

각 ~마다	for each ~	따지다	to argue over
개념	concept		(a small matter)
개인적	personal	또한	also
계산	calculation	똑바로	straight, upright
고개를 숙이다	to bow	뜻	meaning
관심	interest	~로는	as ~
관심을 가지다	to have interests	마찬가지로	similarly
기대다	to lean on	모임	gathering
기분	feeling	무지개	rainbow
기회	chance	물론이지요.	Of course.
껌	chewing gum	바람직하다	to be desirable
끝나다	to be over, done	반드시 = 꼭	for sure; must
끝내다	to finish	반말	non-honorific language
	(something)	방문하다	to visit
끼어들다	to cut in	법적이다	to be legal
내용	content(s)	사적이다	to be personal
~ 년생	~ year born	사회적 지위	social status
노출	exposure	삼세판	the best of three
눈에 띄다	to stand out,	상징하다	to symbolize
	to attract attention	서양식	the Western style
느끼다	to feel	손을 들다	to raise one's hand(s)
담기다	to be contained	손을 흔들다	to wave one's hand(s)
당황하다	to be flustered	술자리	drinking party
대부분	mostly	숫자	number
대하다	to deal with, treat	습관	custom; habit
1등급	top-grade	신경(을) 쓰다	to pay attention to,
따다	to get, obtain		to care
따라서	accordingly, therefore	신기하다	to be surprising, novel
따르다[1]	to follow	실례	discourtesy
따르다[2]	to pour	실수	mistake

쓰이다	to be used	자기	oneself
씹다	to chew	자세	attitude
아마	maybe	자연스럽게	naturally
아이를 낳다	to give birth to a baby	적당히	moderately
악수	handshake	~ 점	thing, point
알아 두다	to keep in mind	정당	political party
알아내다	to find out, figure out	존댓말	honorific language
어른	(one's) elders; adult	존중하다	to respect
~에 대해서	about	종교	religion
~에 비해서	compare to ~	주의하다	to be cautious, careful
여러 가지	various, many	지지하다	to support
연말	end of the year	집중하다	to concentrate
연수	training	짝수	even number
예를 들어	for example	차이점	difference
예의상	out of courtesy	~ 처럼	like, as if
예의에 어긋나다	to go against manners	처음엔	at first
예절	etiquette	= 처음에는	
완성	completion	체중	body weight
외모	appearance	최고	the best
운전 면허	driver's license	취기	the effects of alcohol
원래	originally	친하다	to be close
월급	salary	칭찬	compliment
윗사람	someone of older or higher status	투표권	right to vote
		특징	characteristics
–으니	formal form of -으니까	특히	especially
의견	opinion	표시하다	to mark, indicate
의미	meaning	표현	expression
이외	besides, except	표현하다	to express
이용	use	학번	the year when one enters a college
이제	now		
인생	(one's) life	해	year
인종	race, ethnic group	혹시	by any chance
입학하다	to enter a school	홀수	odd number

2과 한국에서 즐겨 먹는 음식

Lesson 2 Popular Korean Food

학습 목표

내용
- 음식의 맛을 나타내는 표현 및 사용법을 배운다.
- 음식 소개와 설명, 그리고 조리법 표현을 배운다.

문화
- 대표적 길거리 음식의 종류와 배경을 살펴본다.
- 한국의 다양한 먹거리에 대해 배운다.

즐기다 to enjoy 관련되다 to be related 조리법 cooking method 대표적 typical
길거리 street 종류 type 배경 background 살펴보다 to examine 다양하다 to be various
먹거리 food item

■ 생각해 봅시다

가 ▸▸ 다음 질문에 대해 말해 보세요.

1. 여러분 나라의 대표적인 음식을 서로 소개해 봅시다.

2. 어떤 한국 음식을 먹어 봤습니까? 맛있게 먹어 본 한국 음식은 어떤 것들이 있습니까?

3. 못 먹거나 안 좋아하는 (한국) 음식이 있습니까? 그 이유는 무엇입니까?

4. 외국인에게 인기 있는 한국 음식은 뭐가 있을까요?

5. 한국인이 좋아하는 한국 음식은 어떤 것들이 있을까요?

나 ▸▸ 다음 음식들을 먹어 본 적이 있습니까? 어떤 음식인지 이야기해 봅시다.

계란빵	군고구마	군밤	떡볶이
만두	오징어 구이	찐 옥수수	튀김

계란빵 egg bread 군고구마 roasted sweet potato 군밤 roasted chestnut 떡볶이 stir-fried rice cake with vegetables and spicy sauce 만두 dumpling 오징어 구이 roasted squid 찐 옥수수 steamed corn 튀김 deep-fried food

대화

길거리 음식

민준과 수미가 서울 명동에서 만난다

수미: 민준아, 늦어서 미안해. 오래 기다렸지?

민준: 아니야, 괜찮아. 명동에서 뭘 먹을지 검색하고 있었어. 우리 오늘 저녁에 뭐 먹을까?

수미: 저녁? 근데 나 벌써 배고픈데.

민준: 그래? 나도 출출한데 그럼 우리 저녁 먹기 전에 가볍게 뭐**라도**^{GU2.1} 먼저 먹을까?

수미: 그래. 이 근처에 먹을 게 뭐가 있지? 길에서 파는 간단한 음식이 있을까?

민준: 응. 떡볶이, 붕어빵, 순대, 군만두, 호떡⋯ 많지. 빈대떡은 어때? **구수한**^{GU2.2} 빈대떡에 막걸리 한 잔.

수미: 빈대떡은 광장시장에 가서 먹어야지!

민준: 그건 그렇지. 그럼, 다음에는 광장시장에 가고 오늘은 우리 떡볶이 먹을래?

수미: 너 매운 거 괜찮아?

검색하다 to search 출출하다 to be a little hungry 간단하다 to be simple 붕어빵 carp-shaped bread 순대 Korean sausage 호떡 chewy pancake with sugar filling 빈대떡 mung bean pancake 구수하다 to be of rich flavor 막걸리 Korean raw rice wine

민준: 응, 나 매운 거 잘 먹어. 우리 떡볶이가 맛있는 데로 가자. 이리 가면 큰길에 길거리 음식이 많아.

수미: 어머, 저기 튀김, 계란빵, 오징어 구이, 군밤… 정말 많다. 이건 뭐야?

민준: 응, 알감자. 작은 감자를 구운 거야. 먹어 볼래? 맛있어 보인다.

수미: 응. 이거부터 먹어 보자.

민준: 아저씨, 알감자 한 봉지, 떡볶이 일 인분 주세요.

아저씨: 네, 여기 있습니다.

수미: 와, 맛있겠다. 감사합니다.

민준: 많이 먹어. 이 집 떡볶이 어때?

수미: 응. 떡이 쫄깃쫄깃하고 야채도 많이 들어 있어서 괜찮네.

민준: 떡볶이가 **매콤한데**^{GU2.3} 부드러운 알감자랑 같이 먹으니까 잘 어울린다

수미: 어머, 작은 김밥도 있네. 아저씨, 이 김밥 맛있어요?

호떡

알감자

이리 = 이쪽으로 this way   알감자 baby potatoes   굽다 to roast, bake   일 인분 a serving for one   쫄깃쫄깃하다 to be chewy   매콤하다 to be a bit spicy   부드럽다 to be smooth, soft   어울리다 to go well

아저씨: 아, 네. 마약 김밥이요? 맛있어서 한 개만은 못 먹는다고 이름
　　　　이 마약 김밥이에요. 한입에 들어가**도록**^{GU2.4} 작게 만들었죠.

수미: 이름이 재미있네요. 하나만 먼저 먹어 볼게요. 얼마예요?

민준: 잠깐, 마약 김밥은 정말 중독될 정도로 맛있어서 한 개만은
　　　　못 먹고 계속 먹게 될 거야. 아저씨, 이 인분 주세요.

아저씨: 아, 네. 8,000원 되겠습니다.

수미: 내가 살게.

민준: 그래. 자, 10개니까 5개**씩**^{GU2.5} 나눠 먹자.

수미: 이거 정말 맛있다!

민준: 야, **그만 먹어**^{GU2.6}! 우리 저녁도 먹어야 돼.

수미: 알아. 근데 맛있어서 자꾸 손이 가네. 나, 벌써 마약 김밥에
　　　　중독됐나 봐. 하하.

민준: 이따가 저녁 때 포장마차에 가자. 포장마차에 가면
　　　　따끈한^{GU2.7} 음식도 먹을 수 있어. 잔치국수 한 그릇 사 줄게.

수미: 좋아. 오늘 나 정말 배 터지겠다.

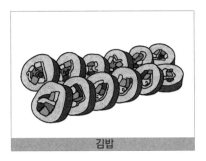

김밥

마약 drugs, narcotics　한입 a single bite　중독되다 to become addicted　나눠 먹다 to share
food　~씩 each　짓다 to form　손이 가다 to reach with one's hand (to eat something)
포장마차 covered street cart bar　따끈하다 to be warm　잔치국수 party noodle dish　터지다
to burst

이해 문제

가... 다음 내용이 대화의 내용과 같으면 ○, 다르면 X에 표시하세요.

1. 민준은 저녁 먹고 나서 길거리 음식을 먹자고 했다.　　　○　　X

2. 떡볶이는 길거리 음식이다.　　　○　　X

3. 녹두 빈대떡은 구수하다.　　　○　　X

4. 수미와 민준은 오늘 빈대떡을 먹을 것이다.　　　○　　X

5. 수미는 매운 음식을 잘 먹는다.　　　○　　X

6. 마약 김밥에는 마약이 들어 있다.　　　○　　X

나... 다음 질문에 대답해 보세요.

1. 민준은 수미를 기다리면서 무엇을 하고 있었습니까?

2. 빈대떡으로 유명한 곳은 어디입니까?

3. 빈대떡과 어울리는 음식은 무엇입니까?

4. 수미와 민준은 명동에서 무슨 음식을 사 먹었습니까?

5. 마약 김밥을 작게 만든 이유는 무엇입니까?

문법과 용법

GU2.1

~(이)라도 'even, at least'

우리 저녁 먹기 전에 간단하게 뭐**라도** 먼저 먹자.

Before eating dinner, let's eat something even if it is something simple.

다른 음료수가 없는데 물**이라도** 마셔.

Since there is no other beverage, at least drink some water.

드디어 주말인데 극장에**라도** 갈까?

It is a finally the weekend. Should we at least go to a theater?

▶ This pattern is structurally composed of the copula stem 이- (which becomes silent after a vowel), the statement ending ~라, the "concessive" particle ~도 'although, but'. Its literal meaning is thus 'although it is …'. It has derived from ~(이)라고 해도 'although (they) say that it is …' with the deletion of –고 하– '(they) say that'. ~(이)라도 is so fossilized that it now functions like a particle to mean 'even' or 'at least (although not the best option)'.

▶ ~(이)라도 is preceded by a noun, a pronoun, a noun phrase, an adverb (e.g., 늦게라도 'even though it is late'), a connective clause (e.g., 돈을 주면서라도 'even by giving money'). It can also be preceded by a particle as in ~에라도, ~에서라도, ~한테라도, ~까지라도, ~부터라도, etc.

> GU2.2

구수하다/고소하다 'to be toasty, flavorful, savory'

나는 오늘 점심으로 **구수한** 녹두 빈대떡이 먹고 싶어.

I want to have savory mung bean *pindaettŏk* for today's lunch.

비빔밥에 참기름을 넣었더니 냄새가 참 **고소해졌다**.

After I had put sesame oil in the *pibimpap*, the aroma became really savory.

할머니의 옛날이야기는 **구수하다**.

Grandmother's fairy tales are nice and pleasant.

▶ 구수하다/고소하다 are adjectives of taste and smell. Its exact meaning is difficult to be rendered in English but roughly is 'to be delicious with a rich, nutty, roasted taste, flavor, smell, aroma, or feel'. These words are used to describe taste or smell. 구수하다 and 고소하다 are a synonymous sound symbolic pair, with a slight difference in feeling or connotation. 구수하다 contains the dark vowel ㅜ and gives the feeling of 'strong, big, and deep', while 고소하다 contains the light vowel ㅗ and gives the feeling of 'delicate, small, and cute'. Thus, 구수하다 goes with 된장찌개 'bean paste stew', 보리차 'barley tea', 누룽지 'crust of overcooked rice', etc., while 고소하다 usually describes 볶은 깨 'roasted sesame', 참기름 'sesame oil', and such.

▶ The expressions can also be used in metaphorical senses to express one's affect. 구수하다 often describes stories and people as in 구수한 옛날이야기 'a delightful fairy tale' and 구수한 사람 'a pleasant person'. On the other hand, 고소하다 describes having schadenfreude, or feeling a satisfaction with a slight guilt over someone getting a due punishment. An example sentence would be 나를 괴롭히던 반 친구가 선생님께 야단을 맞아 고소하다 'A classmate who was bothering me, was scolded by the teacher, so I felt s/he got what s/he deserved'.

> **GU2.3**

> 매콤하다 'to be somewhat spicy hot';
> 달콤하다 'to be somewhat sweet'

된장찌개에 고추를 넣으니까 **매콤하**네요.

Since we put red pepper in the *twenjang-tchigae*, it tastes a little spicy.

제주도 귤이 **새콤달콤하다**.

The Jeju tangerines are somewhat lemony and sweet.

▶ The suffix –콤 is added to several adjectives of taste, typically 맵다 'be spicy hot', 달다 'be sweet', and 새– (derived from 시다 'be sour' due to vowel harmony with 콤, as in 시큼하다 vs. 새콤하다), giving the feel of moderately spicy hot or peppery, moderately sweet, and moderately sour, respectively. Like in English, 달콤하다 can describe feelings and memories such as 달콤한 사랑, 달콤한 추억 'sweet love, sweet memories'.

> **GU2.4**

> ~도록 'so that, to an extent that, until'

저는 건강해지**도록** 매일 운동해요.

I exercise everyday, so that I will become healthy.

오늘은 발이 아프**도록** 하루 종일 걸어다녔다.

Today I walked around all day to the extent that my feet hurt.

해가 뜨**도록** 잤어요.

I slept until sunrise.

▶ The connective ending –도록 is attached to a verb or adjective to express the meaning of purpose, result, or extent. No tense suffix can precede the ending.

▶ -도록 can be followed by the verb 하다 'do' to form the pattern ~도록 하다 'make/ be sure'. Examples include 내일 아침 일찍 오도록 하세요 'Please be sure to come early tomorrow morning' and 조심하도록 하겠습니다 'I will make sure I am more careful'. When used in requests or commands, ~도록 하다 often expresses politeness (e.g., 술은 조금만 마시도록 해 is politer than 술은 조금만 마셔).

GU2.5

~씩 'each, apiece, respectively, per, at a time'

붕어빵과 알감자를 한 봉지**씩** 사자.

Let's buy one bag each of the carp-shaped bread and roasted baby potatoes.

저는 매일 여덟 시간**씩** 잡니다.

I sleep eight hours per day.

▶ The suffix –씩 expresses allocated amount or numbers, or frequency, indicating an idea of regularity or even distribution. That is, –씩 is attached after the word denoting the thing that is being evenly distributed. A numeral followed by a counter usually precedes –씩, as in, 한 봉지씩 'one bag of each, one bag at a time, one bag per person', 두 권씩 'two books apiece', and 만 원씩 'ten thousand won each'. Other words with –씩 include quantity expressions 반(반)씩 'half for each person, half by half', 조금씩 'little by little, little at a time', 이만큼씩 'this much each' referring to quantity; and frequency expressions 가끔씩 'every once in a while' and 이따금씩 'every now and then'. Some question words include 얼마씩 'how much apiece', 몇 (개)씩 'how many apiece', etc.

그만 + verb 'stop doing, don't (do) anymore'

너무 배가 불러서 **그만 먹**을래요.

I am too stuffed so I am going to stop eating.

내일 일찍 학교 가야 하니까 그만 **공부하고** 가서 자라.

Since you have to go to school early tomorrow, stop studying and go to sleep.

▶ The adverb 그만 means 'that amount only, to that extent, no more than that'. When followed by a verb it means to stop the ongoing action denoted by the verb, as in 그만 울어라 'Stop crying; do not cry anymore' (*lit.* 'cry no more than that').

따끈하다 'to be fairly hot, adequately hot (to the touch)'; 따뜻하다 'to be warm'

따끈한 커피 한 잔 주세요.

Please give me a cup of hot coffee.

이번 겨울은 다른 겨울보다 **따뜻해**요.

This winter is warmer than past winters.

이걸 마시면 몸이 **따뜻해**질 거야.

If you drink this, your body will become nice and warm.

▶ A number of adjectives express temperature. While the adjective 뜨겁다 means 'to be hot, heated', 따끈하다 expresses a moderately or adequately hot temperature of objects one can feel by the sense of touch, such as food and beverage. The expression can also be used in repetition for emphasis, as in 따끈따끈하다.

▶ The adjective 따뜻하다 means 'to be warm and nice'. Unlike 따끈하다, it is used to express a pleasantly warm feeling. Furthermore, the cause of the warmth felt can be not only tangible objects, but also intangible state of warmth one perceives as the weather, temperature, atmosphere, emotion, character, and attitude (e.g., 따뜻한 마음 'a warm heart', 따뜻한 환영 'a cordial welcome', 따뜻한 친절 'warm-hearted hospitality', and 따뜻한 사람 'a kindhearted person'). Unlike 따끈하다, 따뜻하다 is not used in repetition like 따뜻따뜻하다.

▶ With the suffix –어지/–아지 'become', 따뜻하다 expresses the change of state to become warm, as in 햇빛이 비치자 방 안은 점점 따뜻해졌다 'With the sun shining in, the room gradually grew warmer'.

활동

가... 주어진 단어에 가장 어울리는 표현을 한 개 고르세요.

1. 떡볶이 —

   ㄱ. 쫄깃쫄깃하다   ㄴ. 달콤하다   ㄷ. 새콤하다   ㄹ. 시원하다

2. 김치찌개 —

   ㄱ. 구수하다   ㄴ. 매콤하다   ㄷ. 새콤달콤하다   ㄹ. 쫄깃쫄깃하다

3. 붕어빵 —

   ㄱ. 덥다   ㄴ. 따끈하다   ㄷ. 짜다   ㄹ. 새콤하다

4. 사탕(캔디) —

   ㄱ. 달콤하다   ㄴ. 따끈하다   ㄷ. 매콤하다   ㄹ. 싱겁다

5. 구수하다 —

   ㄱ. 된장찌개   ㄴ. 떡볶이   ㄷ. 붕어빵   ㄹ. 야채

6. 새콤하다 —

   ㄱ. 만두   ㄴ. 고추장   ㄷ. 레몬   ㄹ. 호떡

7. 따끈하다 —

   ㄱ. 샐러드   ㄴ. 튀김   ㄷ. 포장마차   ㄹ. 막걸리

나... 아래 빈 칸에 가장 <u>적당하지 않은</u> 말을 고르세요.

1. 한국에는 _____ 길거리 음식이 있다.

ㄱ. 여러 가지   ㄴ. 많은   ㄷ. 다양한   ㄹ. 넓은

2. 한국 음식은 요즘 미국에서도 인기가 _____ .

ㄱ. 높다   ㄴ. 다양하다   ㄷ. 많다   ㄹ. 있다

3. 광장시장에 가면 빈대떡 _____ 막걸리를 함께 먹는 사람들이 많다.

ㄱ. 하고   ㄴ. 같이   ㄷ. 이랑   ㄹ. 과

다... 밑줄 친 단어와 가장 <u>비슷한</u> 단어를 찾아보세요.

1. 인터넷에서 맛있는 식당을 <u>검색하고</u> 있어요.

ㄱ. 검사하고   ㄴ. 조사하고   ㄷ. 가 보고   ㄹ. 골라 보고

2. 저는 밤 10시쯤 되면 항상 <u>출출해요</u>.

ㄱ. 배가 불러요   ㄴ. 배가 고파요   ㄷ. 피곤해요   ㄹ. 배가 아파요

3. <u>근처</u>에 맛있는 식당이 있어요?

ㄱ. 근방   ㄴ. 이웃   ㄷ. 장소   ㄹ. 동네

라... 주어진 표현을 사용하여 대화를 완성하세요.

1. ~(이)라도

    ㄱ: 주말인데 심심해 죽겠다!

    ㄴ: 그럼, _____ .

2. ~도록

    ㄱ: 내일 발표가 있는데 실수할까 봐 걱정이야.

    ㄴ: _____ 연습을 많이 하세요.

3. 따뜻하다

    ㄱ: 한국에서 경기를 잘 하고 돌아왔어요?

    ㄴ: 네, 친척들이 _____ 환영을 해 주었어요.

4. -씩

    ㄱ: 사과 한 상자를 선물로 받았는데 20개 들어 있어.

    ㄴ: 우리가 5명이니까 _____ .

5. 그만 + verb

    ㄱ: 너무 졸려서 숙제에 집중할 수가 없네.

    ㄴ: _____ 빨리 자.

마... 다음에 대해 함께 이야기해 보세요.

1. 길거리 음식의 특징은 무엇이라고 생각합니까?

2. 빈대떡과 막걸리, 햄버거와 감자튀김처럼 같이 먹으면 어울리는 음식들은 어떤 것들이 있습니까? 이들 음식이 서로 어울리는 이유는 무엇이라고 생각합니까?

3. 크기가 작아서 한입에 먹기 쉬운 음식들로는 어떤 음식들이 있습니까?

4. 다음 음식과 비슷한 여러분 나라의 음식이 있습니까? 조사해서 소개해 봅시다.

　　ㄱ. 김밥　　　　　ㄴ. 만두　　　　　ㄷ. 붕어빵
　　ㄹ. 빈대떡　　　　ㅁ. 순대　　　　　ㅂ. 어묵

5. 여러분 나라에서 흔히 먹는 길거리 음식에는 어떤 것들이 있습니까?

6. 세계의 길거리 음식에는 어떤 것이 있습니까?

읽기

즐겨 찾는^{GU2.8} 길거리 음식

길거리 음식**이란**^{GU2.9} 말 그대로 식당이 아닌 길에서 파는 먹**거리**다.^{GU2.10} 식사보다는 간식에 가깝고 식당 음식에 비해 싸서 부담 없이 먹을 수 있다. 길거리 음식으로는 떡볶이, 붕어빵, 어묵, 순대, 빈대떡 **등**^{GU2.11}이 있다.

떡볶이

떡볶이

떡볶이는 떡과 야채를 섞어 양념하여 볶은 음식으로 맛도 좋고 영양가도 높아서 많은 사람들이 즐겨 먹는다. 원래는 간장으로 간을 해서 맵지 않게 만든 '궁중 떡볶이'가 있는데, 요즘은 고추장을 넣어 매콤하게 만든 떡볶이가 인기이다.

붕어빵과 계란빵

붕어빵

철판 틀에 밀가루 반죽과 단팥을 넣어 굽는 빵을 풀빵이라 하는데 크기, 모양, 재료에 따라 국화빵,

간식 snack 부담 burden 어묵 fish cake 등 etc. 섞다 to mix 양념 seasoning 볶다 to stir-fry 영양가 nutrition 간장 soy sauce 간을 하다 to season with salt or soy sauce 궁중 royal court 고추장 spicy Korean bean paste 철판 틀 metal mold 밀가루 flour 반죽 dough 단팥 sweet red bean 풀빵 bread with filling made stove-top 크기 size 모양 shape 국화 chrysanthemum

계란빵

붕어빵, 호두빵, 계란빵이라고 한다. 팥 **대신**^{GU2.12}
크림을 넣기도 하는데 요즘은 계란이 들어간 계란빵도
있다. 계란빵은 한 대학교 근처에서 처음 시작되었는데
값이 싸고 먹으면 속이 든든해서 특히 학생들에게
인기가 많다. 붕어빵을 **비롯한**^{GU2.13} 풀빵들은 틀을
사용해 같은 모양으로 만들기 때문에 얼굴이 서로 많이
닮은 사람을 '붕어빵'이라고 부른다.

어묵

어묵

어묵은 생선살에 소금, 설탕 등을 넣어 반죽한 것을
찌거나 굽거나 튀긴 음식이다. 일본식 어묵이 부산을
통해 들어와 주로 '부산 어묵'으로 알려지면서
유명해졌다. 또, 일본어를 따라 '오뎅'이라고도 한다.
어묵은 소화가 잘 되고 단백질이 많다. 추운 겨울
날씨에 따끈한 어묵 국물을 마시면 몸이 따뜻해진다.

순대

순대

순대는 돼지 창자에 당면이나 찹쌀과 야채, 선지를
채운 다음 쪄서 익힌 음식으로 서양의 소시지와
비슷하다. 19세기에 손님을 대접했던 고급 요리라는
기록이 있다. 강원도에서는 돼지 창자 대신 오징어를

호두 walnut 속이 든든하다 stomach to be full 생선살 fish fillets 찌다 to steam 튀기다 to
deep-fry 통하다 to go through 주로 mostly, mainly 소화 digestion 단백질 protein 국물
soup, broth 창자 intestines 당면 sweet potato noodle; glass noodle 찹쌀 glutinous rice,
sticky rice 선지 clotted blood from slaughtered cows and pigs 채우다 to fill 익히다 to
cook 대접 reception, treatment 고급 high quality 기록 record

오징어 순대

사용하여 오징어 순대를 만든다. 함경도에서 강원도 속초로 내려온 사람들이 돼지 창자를 구하기가 어려워 오징어로 순대를 만들어 먹은 게 시작이라고 한다.

빈대떡

빈대떡은 녹두를 갈아서 나물과 고기를 넣어 기름에 부쳐 만드는 음식이다. 녹두는 비타민과 철분이 많다. 빈대떡은 기름에 바삭하게 구워서 맛이 고소하다. 예전에는 손님을 대접할 때에 특히 많이 만들었다는데 지금은 술안주로도 인기가 높다. 서울 광장시장에 가면 막걸리와 빈대떡을 함께 먹는 사람들을 볼 수 있다.

빈대떡

막걸리

한국의 길거리 음식은 다양하고 최근에는 고급화되어 가는 경향도 보인다. 또, 길거리 음식들이 이제는 한국인들뿐만 아니라 외국인들에게도 큰 인기를 얻고 있다. 한국을 방문했을 때 여러 가지 길거리 음식을 먹어 보는 것은 여행에 재미를 더해 줄 것이다.

대신 instead of 녹두 mung bean 갈다 to grind 나물 wild greens 기름 oil 부치다 to pan-fry 철분 iron 고소하다 to have rich flavor (술)안주 snack served with alcoholic beverages 최근에 lately 고급화 to become of a higher quality 경향 trend 재미를 더하다 to add fun

이해 문제

가... 다음 내용이 본문의 내용과 같으면 ○, 다르면 X에 표시하세요.

1. 원래 떡볶이는 안 매운 음식이었다.　　　　　　　　○　　　X

2. 붕어빵은 생선살로 만들었다.　　　　　　　　　　　○　　　X

3. 계란빵은 한 대학교 근처에서 시작되었다.　　　　　○　　　X

4. 어묵은 추운 겨울에 많이 먹는다.　　　　　　　　　○　　　X

5. 순대는 강원도에서 시작되었다.　　　　　　　　　　○　　　X

6. 빈대떡에는 팥을 갈아 넣었다.　　　　　　　　　　　○　　　X

나... 다음 질문에 대답해 보세요.

1. 요즘 흔히 먹는 떡볶이와 원래의 떡볶이 맛의 차이를 설명해 보세요.

2. 풀빵의 종류를 쓰고 특징을 설명해 보세요.

3. 어묵은 어떻게 만든 음식입니까?

4. 한식의 순대는 서양의 어떤 음식과 비슷합니까?

5. 오징어 순대는 어떻게 만들게 되었는지 그 배경을 써 보세요.

6. 빈대떡에 들어가는 재료는 무엇입니까?

7. 막걸리는 어떤 술입니까?

문법과 용법

GU2.8

즐겨 + verb   'enjoy ...ing'

떡볶이는 많은 사람들이 **즐겨 먹**는 간식이다.

Ttŏkbokki is a snack many people enjoy eating.

저는 평소에는 청바지를 **즐겨 입**어요.

I usually like to wear blue jeans.

▶ 즐기다 means 'to enjoy', and it can be combined with other verbs in 즐겨~
(<즐기+어) form to mean 'to enjoy doing something' or 'to do something often'.
Examples include 즐겨 먹다 'enjoy eating (often)', 즐겨 읽다 'read often', 즐겨
하다 'do often', 즐겨 쓰다 'use often', 즐겨 부르다 'sing often'.

GU2.9

~(이)란   'as for (the definition of)'

길거리 음식**이란** 길에서 파는 음식이다.

'Street food' means food sold on streets.

행복**이란** 무엇인가?

What is 'happiness'?

▶ The topic particle (이)란 is an abbreviated form of ~(이)라고 하는 것은 'something called to be ~' with the deletion of 고 하는 것 'something called', while retaining the copula (이), statement ending –라, and the contracted topic particle ㄴ (< 은). The abbreviated form retains the source meaning in a diluted manner. The function of (이)란 is similar to that of the topic particle 은/는. The expression is often used to draw attention to the preceding noun before defining it or providing an explanation.

GU2.10

~거리 'material, stuff, things, source, topic'

길거리 음식이란 식당이 아닌 길에서 파는 먹**거리**다.
'Street foods' are types of food sold on the streets rather than in restaurants.

우리는 곧 이야깃**거리**가 끊어졌어요.
We quickly ran out of conversation topics.

▶ The bound noun 거리 is combined mainly with nouns such as 반찬거리 'ingredients for side dishes', 먹(을)거리 'things to eat', 구경거리 or 볼거리 'things to see', 일거리 'task to be done', 웃음거리 'the butt of jokes', 뉴스거리 'news materials', 걱정거리 'things to worry about', 논문거리 'topic for an article or a dissertation'. It is also combined with modifier forms of some selected verbs, as in 놀 거리 'things to play with', 즐길 거리 'things to enjoy', and 생각할 거리 'something to think about'. Notice that the modifier ending is always ~(으)ㄹ.

GU2.11

등 'etcetera (etc.), and the like, and so on'

길거리 음식으로는 떡볶이, 빈대떡 **등**이 있다.

For street food, there are *ttŏkpokki*, *pindaettŏk*, etc.

저는 주말에는 청소하거나 빨래하는 **등** 보통 혼자서 보내요.

I usually spend the weekends by myself cleaning, doing laundry, and so on.

▶ The Sino-Korean bound noun 등 is used at the end of a list of items when the list is not exhaustive, as in 사과나 배 등을 샀다 'I bought apples, pears, and whatnot'. Unlike placing a comma before "etc." in English, no comma is used before 등.

▶ As 등 is a noun, it can be preceded by a predicate in the modifier form. In this case, the modifier ending must be the present tense form ~는.

GU2.12

~대신(에) 'instead of ...'

슈퍼에는 지금 가는 **대신에** 저녁 먹고 가자.

Instead of going now, let's go to the supermarket after dinner.

시간이 있으면 게임 **대신(에)** 공부를 해라.

If you have time, instead of playing games go study.

▶ The Sino-Korean noun 대신 'substitution' can be combined with the particle 에 'at/on/to/for' to mean 'in place of, on behalf of, instead of'. The particle 에 can be omitted without meaning change. A noun or pronoun usually precedes 대신. A verb may also occur before 대신 in the modifier form, as in 우는 대신(에) 웃었다 '(She) laughed instead of crying'.

~을/를 or 에서 비롯한/비롯하여
'including, headed by, starting with'

풀빵은 붕어빵**을 비롯하여** 여러 종류가 있다.

There are many types of filled breads, including carp-shaped bread.

오늘 행사에는 시장**을 비롯한** 공무원들이 많이 참석했다.

There were many public officers present at today's event including the mayor.

▶ When 비롯하다 is preceded by the object particle 을/를, it means 'including', etc. and is used only in the form ~을/를 비롯하여 or ~을/를 비롯한, and not as the main verb of a sentence. Thus, ~을/를 비롯했다 is unacceptable.

▶ The basic meaning of the verb 비롯하다 is 'to begin, start, originate, arise (from)'. In this meaning, the verb occurs with the preceding particle 에서 'from', as in 싸움은 작은 오해에서 비롯하였다 'The fight originated from a small misunderstanding'.

활동

가... 아래 빈 칸에 가장 적당한 말을 고르세요.

1. 길거리 음식_____ 길에서 파는 간식을 말한다.

　　ㄱ. 이란　　　　　ㄴ. 으로는　　　　ㄷ. 대신　　　　ㄹ. 마다

2. 오늘은 윤 선생님 _____ 정 선생님이 수업을 하실 거예요.

　　ㄱ. 함께　　　　　ㄴ. 대신　　　　ㄷ. 등　　　　ㄹ. 이란

3. 이번 공연에는 빅뱅을 _____ 많은 K-pop 가수들이 나온다.

　　ㄱ. 비롯한　　　ㄴ. 다양한　　　ㄷ. 선호한　　　ㄹ. 비교한

4. 이 사진의 음식들은 정말로 맛있어 _____.

　　ㄱ. 보인다　　　ㄴ. 같다　　　ㄷ. 생겼다　　　ㄹ. 죽겠다

5. 시원한 맥주와 치킨은 정말 잘 _____.

　　ㄱ. 가요　　　　ㄴ. 어울려요　　　ㄷ. 먹어요　　　ㄹ. 맞춰요

나... 다음의 주어진 표현을 넣어서 문장을 만들어 보세요.

1. ~ noun (이)란

　　ㄱ. 사랑 _____.

　　ㄴ. 행복 _____.

2. 등

ㄱ. 길거리 음식으로는 _____이 있습니다.

ㄴ. 대통령은 _____ 방문한다.

3. ~을/를 비롯하여

ㄱ. 커피숍 메뉴에는 _____이/가 있습니다.

ㄴ. 오늘 회의에 _____이/가 왔습니다.

다... 다음 질문에 대해 이야기해 봅시다.

1. 여러분이 좋아하는 한국 음식은 주로 어디에서 먹습니까?

2. 다음 음식을 서로에게 설명해 보고 무슨 음식인지 맞혀 보세요.

계란빵	김밥	떡볶이	만두
오징어 구이	붕어빵	빈대떡	순대
어묵	알감자	찐 옥수수	호떡

3. 교과서에 나오지 않은 한국의 길거리 음식에 대해 인터넷에서 검색해 보고 어떤 음식들인지 이야기해 보세요.

4. 포장마차가 무엇인지 조사해서 한 문단으로 써 보세요.

5. 여러분이 좋아하는 음식을 골라 조리법과 맛을 설명하는 글을 하나 써 보세요.

외국인이 뽑은 한국 음식

최근 서울시가 외국인 1,984명을 대상으로 '외국인이 뽑은 한국 음식'을 설문 조사한 결과 삼겹살이 가장 선호하는 음식으로 나타났다. 2위는 김치 요리, 3위는 떡볶이가 차지했다. 또, 일본인들 중에서는 삼계탕이 1위였다. 이 밖에 의외로 된장찌개가 영어권 외국인들에게 인기가 높았고, 순대나 호떡 등 길거리 음식을 좋아한다는 의견도 많았다.

치맥

전통 한국 요리 중 닭 요리로는 삼계탕과 닭볶음탕이 있다. 서양식 닭 요리는 흔히 프라이드 치킨이라고 하는데 전통 한국 음식은 아니다. 한국에서는 1960년대에 통닭 가게가 생겼고, 그 후 맥줏집과 함께 치킨집이 많아졌다. 즉, 치킨이 술 안주로 인기를 얻은 것이다.

올림픽이나 월드컵 등 큰 스포츠 경기가 있으면 치킨과 맥주를 배달시켜 먹으면서 TV를 보는 사람들이 많다. 치킨과 맥주를 합쳐서 "치맥"이라는 말이 만들어졌고, 이것은 한국 드라마를 통해서 다른 나라에서까지 유행하게 되었다. 또, '치맥 페스티벌'도 생겼다. 많은 사람들이 페스티벌에 갔고, 사람들이 치킨과 맥주를 많이 사면서 치맥 관련 회사의 주가가 올라갔다고 한다.

설문 조사 survey 선호하다 to prefer 요리 cooked dish 차지하다 to be ranked 이 밖에 besides 의외로 unexpectedly 영어권 English-speaking regions 인기가 높다 to be popular 흔히 commonly 통닭 roasted whole-chicken 맥주 beer 합치다 to combine 주가 stock price

팥빙수

한국인의 여름 디저트로 가장 인기 있는 빙수는 토핑에 따라 그 맛과 종류가 다양한데 팥을 넣은 팥빙수가 있고, 과일을 넣은 과일 빙수도 있다. 다음은 더운 여름에 집에서도 간단히 만들어 먹을 수 있는 팥빙수 만드는 법이다.

[재료]

얼음, 단팥 1캔, 꿀 1 스푼, 빙수떡, 시럽, 연유(또는 우유) 3스푼
과일, 아이스크림, 시리얼

[만드는 법]

1. 단팥을 꿀과 섞는다.

2. 얼음을 갈아 그릇에 담는다.

3. 갈아 놓은 얼음 위에 연유나 우유를 넣는다.

4. 그 위에 팥을 올려 놓는다.

5. 마지막으로 시리얼을 약간 뿌리고, 아이스크림과 과일, 빙수떡을 올려 완성한다.

6. 기호에 따라 인절미 떡이나 견과류를 넣어도 된다.

팥빙수 shaved ice with sweet red beans 토핑 topping 재료 ingredients 얼음 ice 캔 can
스푼 spoon 꿀 honey 시럽 syrup 연유 condensed milk 시리얼 breakfast cereal 그릇
bowl or dish 뿌리다 to sprinkle 완성하다 to complete 기호 preference 견과류 nuts

▪▪ 번역문 ▪▪

CONVERSATION: Street Food in Myeong-dong

Minjun and Sumi meet in Seoul's Myeong-dong.

Sumi: Minjun, sorry I'm late. You must have waited a long time, didn't you?

Minjun: Ah, no it's fine. I was looking-up what to eat in Myeong-dong. What should we have for dinner tonight?

Sumi: Dinner? But, I'm already hungry.

Minjun: Ah really? I'm a bit hungry, too. Then, should we have something light before dinner.

Sumi: Okay. What's there to eat around here? Is there simple street food?

Minjun: Yes. *Ttŏkpokki* (rice cake stir-fry), *pungŏ-ppang* (carp-shaped pastry with filling), *sundae* (sausage), *kun-mandoo* (pan-fried dumpling), or *hottŏk* (sugar-filled pancake) … there are a lot. How about *pindaettŏk* (mung bean pancake)? That would be a savory *pindaettŏk* with a glass of *makkŏlli* (Korean rice wine).

Sumi: For *pindaettŏk*, you have to go and eat at Gwangjang Market!

Minjun: That is true. Then how about if we go to Gwangjang Market next time, and have *ttŏkpokki* today?

Sumi: Are you okay with spicy food?

Minjun: Yeah, I can eat spicy food. Let's go to a place with good *ttŏkpokki*. If we go this way, there's a big road with a lot of street food.

Sumi: Wow. There are *t'wigim* (fried food), *kyeran-ppang* (*lit.* egg bread), *ojingŏ kui* (grilled squid), *kwunbam* (roasted chestnuts)…there really are a lot! What are these?

Minjun: Yeah, *algamja* (baby potatoes). They're roasted small potatoes. Do you want to try them? They look delicious.

Sumi: Yes, let's eat these first.

Minjun: *Ajŏssi* (*lit.* Uncle, an English equivalent of "Sir"), please give us one bag of *algamja* and one serving of *ttŏkpokki*.

Vendor: Yes, here they are.

Sumi: Wow, they look delicious. Thank you.

Minjun: Let's eat. (*Lit.* Eat a lot.) How's the *ttŏkpokki* at this place?

Sumi: Yeah, it's not bad, the rice cakes are chewy, and there are a lot of vegetables too.

Minjun: *Ttŏkpokki* is a bit spicy, but it goes together well when you eat them with *al-gamja*.

Sumi: Wow, here are also small *kimbap*. *Ajŏssi* (*lit.* Uncle), are these *kimbap* good?

Vendor: Oh, you mean the *mayak kimbap*? Its name is *mayak* (*lit.* narcotics) *kimbap* because they say that it is so delicious that you cannot eat just one. It is made small, so you can eat one in a single bite.

Sumi: That is a fun name. Let me just try one first. How much is it?

Minjun: Wait, the *mayak kimbap* really is so good to the point that you could become addicted. So, you won't be able to have just one but will keep eating. *Ajŏssi*, can you give us two servings?

Vendor: Oh, yes. That will be 8,000 won.

Sumi: It's on me.

Minjun: Okay. Now since there are ten, let's split it five pieces each.

Sumi: These taste really good!

Minjun: Hey, stop eating! We have to have dinner, too.

Sumi: I know. But these are so good that I can't stop reaching for more. I guess I'm already addicted to (the drug) *mayak kimbap*. Ha ha.

Minjun: Let's go to a street vending cart later in the evening. You can eat hot food when you go to the covered carts. I'll buy you a bowl of party noodles.

Sumi: All right. I'm going to be really stuffed today.

READING: Street Food Everyone Enjoys

Street food is, as the name would suggest, food sold on streets rather than in restaurants. Street food is closer to being a snack rather than a meal, and because the price is low when compared to food sold at restaurants, almost anybody can afford to eat it (*lit.* eat without a burden). Street food includes *ttŏkpokki* (rice cake stir-fry), *pungŏ-*

ppang (carp-shaped pastry with filling), *ŏmuk* (fish cake), *sundae* (sausage), and *pindaettŏk* (mung bean pancake).

1. *Ttŏkpokki* (Rice Cake with Vegetables and Spicy Sauce)

Ttŏkpokki is a dish made by stir-frying a mix of vegetables with Korean rice cake. Because it is tasty and nutritious, many people enjoy the dish. There originally was *kungjung ttŏkpokki* (*lit.* royal rice cake stir-fry) which is seasoned with soy sauce and was not spicy. However, these days, *ttŏkpokki* made spicy with spicy *koch'ujang* (*lit.* chili pepper paste) is popular.

2. *Pungŏ-ppang* and *Kyeran-ppang* (*lit.* Carp Bread and Egg Bread)

Bread that is baked by putting dough and sweet red beans in a metal cast rather than an oven is called *p'ulppang*. Depending on the shape and ingredients used to make *p'ulppang*, it may be called *kuk'wa-ppang* (chrysanthemum bread), *pungŏ-ppang* (carp bread), *hodu-ppang* (walnut bread), and *kyeran-ppang* (egg bread). *Kyeran-ppang* first started near a university. *Kyeran-ppang* is especially popular amongst students because it is cheap and it fills you up when you eat it. Because *p'ulppang*, including carp bread, is made by using metal casts, all of which are of the same shape, people who have similar faces are called '*pungŏ-ppang*'.

3. *Ŏmuk* (Fish Cake)

Fish cake is a food made by putting things like salt and sugar in fish fillets and mixing them together into a dough, then they are steamed, baked, or fried. Japanese style fish cake came into the country through Busan, and it became popular while being referred to mostly as Busan *ŏmuk* (*lit.* fish cake). Also, it is frequently called '*odeng*', following the Japanese name. Fish cake is easy to digest and is high in protein. In cold winter weather, one can warm up by drinking warm fish cake soup.

4. *Sundae* (Korean Sausage)

Korean sausage, or *sundae* (pronounced like "soon-dae"), is similar to Western sausage and is made by putting glass noodles or glutinous rice along with vegetables and *sŏnji* (hardened blood) inside of pig intestines, and then steaming the intestines until they are cooked. There are records indicating that in the 19th century, *sundae* was a gourmet dish served to guests. In Gangwon Province rather than using pig intestines, squid is used to make *ojingŏ sundae* (squid sausage). It is said that *ojingŏ sundae* originated from people who moved down from Hamgyong Province (North Korea) to Sokcho in Gangwon Province (South Korea) were not able to acquire pig intestines easily and began using squid to make sausage.

5. *Pindae-ttŏk* (Mung Bean Pancake)

Pindae-ttŏk, or mung bean pancake, is made by pureeing mung beans and then putting in herbs and meat before pan-frying it in oil. Mung beans are high in vitamins and iron. The mung bean pancake has a rich flavor because it is cooked in oil until crispy. In the past, the mung bean pancake was made often, especially when entertaining guests, and today it is a popular side dish served with alcohol. If you go to Gwangjang Market in Seoul, you can see people eating mung bean pancake along with *makkŏlli*, Korean liquor.

Korean street food has a wide variety and shows the tendency to be of a higher quality, too. Various street foods in Korea are now gaining popularity not only among Koreans, but also among foreigners. When visiting Korea, eating a variety of street food will add to the fun of traveling.

FURTHER READINGS: Food That Foreigners Picked

Recently, the Seoul Metropolitan Government surveyed 1,984 foreign residents and the results showed that the food they preferred the most was pork belly. In second place was kimchi dishes, and in third place was spicy rice cake stir-fry with vegetables. Also, *samgyet'ang* or stuffed chicken soup was the most popular among Japanese people. In addition, *toenjang-tchigae*, Korean bean paste stew, was surprisingly popular among foreigners from English-speaking countries, and there were many opinions given showing that they liked street food such as Korean sausage or *sundae* and pancake with filling or *hottŏk*.

Ch'imaek (Chicken and Beer)

Samgyet'ang, stuffed-chicken soup, and *takpokkŭm-t'ang*, chicken stir-fried stew, are two traditional Korean chicken dishes. Commonly called *p'ŭraidŭ ch'ik'in* (a loan word of fried chicken), it is a Western-style chicken dish and is not a traditional Korean food.

In Korea, rotisserie chicken restaurants were first introduced in the 1960s, followed by a growing number of beer pubs and chicken restaurants. In other words, chicken became a popular bar food.

During the Olympics and the World Cup soccer competitions, many people would have chicken and beer, or *ch'imaek*, delivered to eat while they watch games on TV. The newly-coined term *ch'imaek* was formed, and the term became popular in other countries through Korean dramas is an acronym for *ch'ik'in* for chicken and *maekchu* for beer in Korean. The 'Ch'imaek Festival' also emerged. Many people attended the festival, and because they bought so much chicken and beer, they say that the stock prices of the chicken and beer companies went up.

CULTURE: *P'atbingsu* (Shaved Ice with Sweet Red Beans)

One of the most popular summer dessert items for Koreans is *pingsu*, or shaved ice. Depending on the toppings, there is a variety of flavors and types of *pingsu*. They include *p'atbingsu* with red beans, and *kwail* (fruit) *pingsu*, which has fruits added.

The following is a sweet red bean shaved ice recipe that one can easily follow to make *p'atbingsu* at home in the hot summer.

Ingredients: ice, 1 can of sweet red beans, 1 spoon of honey, rice cake pieces made specifically for *pingsu*, syrup, 3 spoons of condensed milk (or milk), fruit, ice cream, cereal

1. Mix red beans with honey.
2. Shave ice, and place it in a bowl.
3. Add condensed milk or milk to shaved ice.
4. Place red beans on top of the shaved ice.
5. Lastly, sprinkle a little bit of cereal on top and add ice cream, fruit, and rice cake to finish.
6. According to your preference, you may add nuts or soft rice cake coated with bean flour.

▰▰ 단어 ▰▰

간단하다	to be simple	단백질	protein
간식	snack	단팥	sweet red bean
간을 하다	to season with salt or soy sauce	당면	sweet potato noodle; glass noodle
간장	soy sauce	~대신	instead of …
갈다	to grind	대접	reception, treatment
검색하다	to search	대표적	typical
경향	trend	등	etcetera, etc.
계란빵	egg bread	따끈하다	to be warm
고급	high quality	떡볶이	stir-fried rice cake with vegetables and spicy sauce
고급화	to become of a higher quality	마약	drugs, narcotics
고소하다	to have rich flavor	막걸리	traditional Korean rice wine
고추장	spicy Korean bean paste		
관련되다	to be related	만두	dumpling
구수하다	to be of rich flavor	매콤하다	to be a bit spicy
국물	soup, broth	먹거리	food item
국화	chrysanthemum	모양	shape
군고구마	roasted sweet potato	밀가루	flour
군밤	roasted chestnut	반죽	dough
굽다	to roast; to bake	배경	background
궁중	royal court	볶다	to stir-fry
기록	record	부담	burden
기름	oil	부드럽다	to be smooth, soft
기호	preference for, taste	부치다	to pan-fry
길거리	street	붕어빵	carp-shaped bread
나눠 먹다	to share food	빈대떡	mung bean pancake
나물	wild greens	살펴보다	to examine
녹두	mung bean	삼겹살	pork belly meat
다양하다	to be various	생선살	fish fillets

섞다	to mix	잔치국수	a party noodle dish
선지	clotted blood from slaughtered cows and pigs	재미를 더하다	to add fun
선호하다	to prefer	조리법	cooking method
설문 조사	survey	종류	type
소화	digestion	주로	mostly, mainly
속이 든든하다	stomach to be full	중독되다	to become addicted
손이 가다	to reach one's hand (to eat something)	즐기다	to enjoy
		짓다	to form
순대	Korean sausage	쫄깃쫄깃하다	to be chewy
~씩	each	찌다	to steam
(술)안주	snack served with alcoholic beverages	차지하다	to be ranked
		찹쌀	glutinous rice, sticky rice
시리얼	breakfast cereal	창자	intestines
알감자	baby potatoes	채우다	to fill
양념	seasoning	철분	iron
어묵	fish cake	철판 틀	metal mold
어울리다	to go well	최근에	lately
영양가	nutrition	출출하다	to be a little hungry
영어권	English-speaking regions	크기	size
오징어 구이	grilled squid	터지다	to burst
요리	cooked dish	통하다	to go through
의견	opinion	튀기다	to deep-fry
의외로	unexpectedly	포장마차	covered street cart bar
이 밖에	besides	풀빵	bread with filling made stove-top
이리 = 이쪽으로	this way		
익히다	to cook	한입	a single bite
인기가 높다	to be popular	호두	walnut
일 인분	a serving for one		

한국의 데이트 문화

Lesson 3 Dating Culture in Korea

학습 목표

내용 • 설문 조사를 분석할 때에 필요한 표현들을 배운다.

• 간접 화법을 정확하고 적절하게 사용할 수 있도록 한다.

문화 • 한국 젊은이들의 데이트 문화를 이해한다.

• 다른 나라의 데이트 문화와 비교해 본다.

설문 조사 survey 분석하다 to analyze 간접 화법 indirect quotation 적절하게
appropriately, properly 젊은이 young people 비교하다 to compare

■ 생각해 봅시다

가 ▶▶ 다음 질문에 대해 같이 이야기해 봅시다.

1. 처음 만남은 어떻게 시작될까요?

2. 보통 몇 살 때 첫 데이트를 시작하는 것 같습니까?

3. '사귀다'의 기준(criteria)은 무엇일까요?

4. 보통 어떤 이유로 헤어집니까?

5. 데이트 장소로 어떤 곳이 인기가 있습니까?

나 ▶▶ 다음 표현들은 연애와 관련된 표현들입니다. 무슨 뜻인지 알아보고 같이 이야기해 봅시다.

1. 소개팅   2. 양다리 걸치다

3. 바람을 피우다   4. 스킨십

5. 어장 관리   6. 썸 타다, 썸녀, 썸남

7. 밀당   8. 모태솔로

9. 금사빠   10. 속도위반

대 화

고민 상담해 주세요!

라디오 연애 상담 프로그램

상담자: 네, 다음 분. 안녕하세요.

청취자: 안녕하세요. 저는 22살이고 서울에 사는 여자예요.

상담자: 네, 무슨 고민이죠?

청취자: 남자 친구가 있는데 요즘 **마음**^{GU3.1}이 식은 것 같아서요.

상담자: 아, 남자 친구가 변한 **것 같다**^{GU3.2}는 말씀이죠?

청취자: 네.

상담자: 얼마 동안 사귀었어요?

청취자: 400일 정도요.

상담자: 400일이요… 남자 친구가 어떻게 하는데요?

청취자: 음…, 많이 차가워졌어요. 남자 친구**라기보다**^{GU3.3} 그냥 아는
오빠**처럼**^{GU3.4} 행동해요.

상담자: 혹시 다른 여자가 있는 건 아닌가요?

청취자: 거의 매일 만났기 때문에 그럴 **리는 없어요.**^{GU3.5}

상담자: 그럼 왜 그러는 것 같아요?

청취자: 모르겠어요. 지난 번에 오빠가 그러더라고요. 저에 대한 마음
이 예전 같지 않고 노력하는데 안 된**다고.**^{GU3.6}

고민 worry, concern 상담 counsel 연애 date 상담자 counselor 청취자 (radio) listener
마음이 식다 to lose interest (in someone) 변하다 to change into 차갑다 (one's attitude) to
be cold 행동하다 to behave 예전 the past 노력하다 to try hard

상담자: 남자 친구가 헤어지자고 했어요?

청취자: 아직 안 했어요. 근데, 제가 먼저 헤어지자고 말하기를 기다리는 것 같아요.

상담자: 그래서 남자 친구한테 뭐라고 하셨어요?

청취자: 마음 정리할 시간이 필요하다고 했고, 지금 한 달 정도 지났어요. 근데, 연락이 없어요.

상담자: 그런 얘기를 들었는**데도**^{GU3.7} 계속 만나고 싶으세요? 연락도 없는데…

청취자: 추억들이 많고…, 정말 행복했었거든요…

상담자: 참 안타깝고, 제 마음도 무거워지네요. 그런데 남자가 그렇게 말했으면 이제는 마음이 없는 거예요. 마음을 바꾸기 힘들어요.

청취자: 근데, 남자 친구가 아직 커플링도 끼고 있고 SNS 프로필 사진도 저하고 같이 있는 사진이고… 그래서 아직 마음이 있는 것 같은데…

상담자: 그건 아직 안 헤어졌으니까 그럴 거예요. 마음이 많이 아프겠지만 자꾸 매달리면 더 힘들고 남자 친구도 더 싫어하실 거예요.

청취자: 그럼 인연이 여기까지라고 생각하고 그냥 놓아 줘야 돼요?

상담자: 걱정할 **것 없어요**.^{GU3.8} 지금은 죽을 것같이 힘들어도 시간이 지나면 다 잊혀질 겁니다. 아직 젊고 할 일도 많으시니까 힘내세요. 좋은 남자 만날 겁니다.

헤어지다 to break up 마음(을) 정리하다 to clear one's mind 추억 recollection, reminiscence
안타깝다 to be sorry; to be pitiful 마음이 무겁다 to have a heavy heart 커플링 matching
rings between lovers 매달리다 to cling to; to beg 인연 affinity; fate 놓아 주다 to let go
잊혀지다 to be forgotten 젊다 to be young, youthful

이해 문제

가... 다음 내용이 대화의 내용과 같으면 ○, 다르면 X에 표시하세요.

   1. 청취자는 요즘 다른 남자가 마음에 들었다.   ○   X

   2. 상담자는 청취자에게 남자 친구하고 헤어지라고 말했다.   ○   X

   3. 청취자는 SNS 때문에 남자 친구하고 크게 싸웠다.   ○   X

   4. 청취자는 남자 친구하고 1년 조금 넘게 사귀었다.   ○   X

   5. 청취자는 남자 친구하고 헤어지고 싶지 않다.   ○   X

나... 다음 질문에 대답해 보세요.

   1. 다음 표현은 무슨 뜻일까요?

      ㄱ. 마음이 예전 같지 않다

      ㄴ. 마음이 있다/없다

      ㄷ. 마음이 식다

      ㄹ. 마음을 정리하다

      ㅁ. 마음이 무겁다

   2. 여러분이 청취자라면 이런 상황에서 어떻게 하겠습니까?

   3. 여러분이 상담자라면 청취자에게 어떻게 하라고 이야기해 주겠습니까?

   4. 남자 친구가 아직도 커플링을 끼고 있고, 프로필 사진도 안 바꾼 이유는 뭐라고
      생각합니까?

   5. 남자 친구나 여자 친구가 마음이 식는 이유는 어떤 것이 있을까요?

문법과 용법

GU3.1

마음 'mind, spirit, feeling, heart, intention'

저는 의대에 가고 싶었는데 요즘은 **마음**이 식었습니다.

I wanted to go to medical school but nowadays I am not really
interested in that anymore.

마음이 아프지만, 이제는 여자 친구에 대한 **마음**을 정리해야겠어요.

My heart aches, but it is time for me to get rid of my feelings for my girlfriend.

▶ 마음, whose basic meaning is 'mind', is one of the most frequently used native
nouns. It combines with various predicates to create idiomatic expressions. Some
examples are 마음이 있다 'be interested in', 마음이 식다 'be cooled off; not be interested in anymore', 마음이 아프다 'feel hurt; one's heart aches', 마음을 정리하다
'(*lit.* to organize mind) clean up one's mind', 마음을 주다 'trust (someone)', 마음에
걸리다 'feel uneasy', 마음에 들다 'be to one's liking', 마음(을) 놓다 'set one's mind
at ease', and 마음(을) 먹다 'have the intention of (doing)'.

GU3.2

~ 는/(으)ㄴ/(으)ㄹ 것 같다 'it seems that ...'

비가 오**는 것 같**네요.

It seems to be raining.

비가 **온 것 같**네요.

It seems to have rained.

내일은 아주 더**울 것 같**아요.

It seems that it will be very hot tomorrow.

수전이 잘못**한 것 같**으니까 수전이 사과해야 돼.

Susan, you have to apologize because you seem to have made a mistake.

▶ This pattern, meaning 'it seems that' or 'it looks like', is composed of a modifier ending, the bound noun 것 'thing, fact', and the adjective 같다 'same, similar, like'. ~는 것 같다 indicates the present tense of the preceding verb; ~ㄴ(은) 것 같다 the past of the preceding verb or the present of the preceding adjective; and ~(으)ㄹ 것 같다 for the future of the preceding verb or adjective. This pattern is very popular in spoken Korean. Sometimes, Koreans use it when it is not needed, as in 나는 목이 아픈 것 같아요 'I think I have a sore throat'.

GU3.3

~다기보다/~라기보다   'rather than, more of ... than'

미아는 학생이**라기보다** 선생님 같아요.

Mia looks like more of a teacher than a student.

저는 머리가 좋**다기보다** 그냥 모든 일에 열심히 하는 거예요.

Rather than being intelligent, I just try hard in everything I do.

▶ This pattern has derived from ~다고/~라고 하기보다 'rather than saying that', with the deletion of –고 하– 'saying that'. Before ~라기보다, only the present form of the copula (이) may occur, while all forms of verbs and adjectives, as well as the past form of the copula may occur before ~다기보다, as in 갔다기보다,

좋았다기보다, and 학생이었다기보다.

GU3.4

~처럼 'like'; ~(와/과) 같이 'like'

우리 선생님은 저희들을 가족**(과) 같이/가족처럼** 대해 주셨어요.
Our teacher treated us like family.

그 아이의 눈은 호수**처럼**/호수**(와) 같이** 맑았다.
The child's eyes were as clear as a lake.

▶ The particles of comparison/contrast 처럼 'like' and (와/과) 같이 'like' have
similar meanings. They are attached to a noun or pronoun and are used
interchangeably, as in 이처럼 'like this' and 이(와) 같이 'like this'. (와/과) 같이
has developed from 와/과 같이 'in the same ways as'. Unlike 처럼, (와/과) 같이 or
just 같이 also means 'together', as in 나는 친구들과 같이 살아요 'I live (together)
with friends' and 우리 같이 가요 'Let's go together'.

GU3.5

~(으)ㄹ 리가 없다 'There is no way…
There is no reason why…'

공부를 하나도 안 했으니 내가 시험을 잘 볼 **리가 없어.**
Since I didn't study at all, there is no way that I can score well on the test.

제니가 너를 싫어할 **리가 없어**.

There is no reason for Jenny to dislike you.

▶ This pattern is used to express disbelief, skepticism or doubt. This pattern is only used in a statement, but ㄹ(을) 리가 있다 can be used in rhetorical questions to mean the same thing as in 제니가 너를 싫어할 리가 있겠어? 'There is no reason for Jenny to dislike you, right?'

GU3.6

~다고; ~냐고; ~자고; ~라고　 Indirect Quotation

Statement	Verb stem ~ㄴ/는다고	• (말)하다
	Adjective stem ~다고	• 그러다
	Copula stem ~라고	• 물어보다
	Past tense ~다고	• (질문)하다
Question	Verb stem ~냐고/~느냐고	
Request/Proposal	Verb stem ~자고	
Command	Verb stem ~(으)라고	

수지가 학교에 간**다고** 했어요.

Susie said that she was going to school.

수지가 저한테 몇 시에 학교에 가**냐고**/가**느냐고** 물어봤어요.

Susie asked me what time I go to school.

(~느냐고 can be added to a verb only, not to an adjective.)

수지가 내일 도서관에서 만나**자고** 했어요.

Susie asked me to meet at the library tomorrow.

선생님은 저한테 계속 열심히 공부하**라고** 그러셨어요.

My teacher told me to keep studying hard.

수지는 지난 학기에 장학금을 받**았다고** 자랑했어요.

Susie bragged that she got a scholarship last semester.

▶ The indirect quotation pattern is used when the speaker quotes what somebody else or the speaker himself/herself said. It is composed of a quoted clause and a main verb of saying. The quoted clause consists of one of the four sentence-type endings in the plain speech level followed by the quotative particle 고 'that'. Many verbs of saying may function as the main verb, but the most common ones are (말)하다 and 그러다.

GU3.7

~는데도 'although, even though, in spite of the fact that ..., despite that ...'

린다는 돈이 없**는데도** 비싼 차를 샀어요.

Linda does not have much money, but still bought an expensive car.

제가 매뉴얼을 여러 번 설명을 했**는데도** 제니는 다 잊어버렸어요.

I explained the manual several times but Jenny forgot everything.

▶ This pattern is the combination of the "background provider" ending ~는데 'in the situation that' and the "concessive" ending ~도 'although, but', thus literally meaning 'although in the situation that'. This usage can be reinforced by adding 불구하고 'in spite of (that/the situation)', as in 린다는 돈이 없는데도

불구하고 비싼 차를 샀어요 'Linda does not have enough money but, in spite of that, she bought an expensive car'.

~(으)ㄹ 것 없다 'there is no need to (do)'

그렇게 화낼 **거 없잖아요**. 제가 잘 몰라서 실수한 건데요.

There no reason for you to get angry. It's just a mistake I made because I didn't know any better.

말해도 듣지 않는 사람한테 뭐 말할 **것(이) 있겠어요?**

What's the use in talking to a person who never listens to others?

▶ This pattern, contracted from ~ㄹ(을) 것이 없다 'there is nothing to (do)', as in 먹을 것이 없다 'there is nothing to eat'. In the idiomatic usage as in this pattern, it means 'there is no need/reason to (do)'. In this pattern, the subject particle 이 is not allowed after 것 and 것 can optionally be contracted to 거.

활동

가... 다음 빈 칸에 가장 어울리는 단어를 고르세요.

1. 친구 어머니가 돌아가셨다는 이야기를 듣고 내 마음이 _____.

   ㄱ. 아팠다   ㄴ. 없었다   ㄷ. 정리했다   ㄹ. 컸다

2. 올해는 매일 운동을 하기로 마음을 _____.

   ㄱ. 식었다   ㄴ. 걸렸다   ㄷ. 먹었다   ㄹ. 주었다

3. 요즘 취직 문제 때문에 고민이 많아서 선생님께 _____을/를 받았다.

   ㄱ. 연애   ㄴ. 상담   ㄷ. 추억   ㄹ. 이별

4. _____에는 중·고등학생이 연애하는 것은 좋지 않게 보았다.

   ㄱ. 연락   ㄴ. 인연   ㄷ. 소개   ㄹ. 예전

5. 내 친구는 노트북을 잃어버려서 그동안 열심히 한 숙제를 제출할 수 없었다.
   정말 _____.

   ㄱ. 안타까웠다   ㄴ. 변했다   ㄷ. 차가웠다   ㄹ. 잊혀졌다

나... 주어진 표현을 사용하여 대화를 완성해 보세요.

1. ~ㄴ(은)/는데도

   ㄱ: 요즘 무슨 고민 있어?

   ㄴ: _____ 성적이 안 올라.

2. ~라기/다기보다

　　ㄱ: 미안해. 나 때문에 화났지?

　　ㄴ: _____ 다른 친구 때문이야.

3. ~것 같다

　　ㄱ: 요즘 미국 경제 상황이 어때요?

　　ㄴ: 일자리가 많아져서 _____.

4. ~다고/라고 하다

　　ㄱ: 지난 학기 한국어 수업 어땠어요?

　　ㄴ: 많은 친구들이 _____.

5. ~ㄹ(을) 것 없다

　　ㄱ: 왜 너는 항상 약속 시간에 늦어서 나를 기다리게 하니?

　　ㄴ: 난 5분밖에 안 늦었는데 _____.

6. ~ㄹ(을) 리(가/는) 없다

　　ㄱ: 나 어제 클럽에서 린다 봤어.

　　ㄴ: 정말? _____ 아프다고 들었는데.

7. ~처럼

　　ㄱ: 스티브 씨는 어떻게 생겼어요?

　　ㄴ: _____ 멋있어요.

다... 다음은 연애에 대한 고민입니다. 여러분이 상담자라면 어떻게 하겠습니까?

1. 저는 5년을 사귄 남자 친구가 있어요. 그런데 두 달 전에 친구 생일 파티에서 한 남자를 알게 되었는데 마음이 가요. 이 남자도 저에게 관심을 보이고 있어요. 그 래서 몇 번 만나서 밥도 먹고 영화도 봤어요. 물론 제 남친은 저에게 정말 좋은 사 람이에요. 아무것도 모르는 남친한테 너무 미안하네요. 어떻게 할까요?

2. 많은 분들이 애인과 헤어진 적이 있지요? 저는 두 달 전에 헤어졌는데 아직 마음 이 많이 아파요. 밥 먹다가도 울고 싶고 헤어진 여자친구한테 전화하고 싶고… 여러분, 헤어져서 마음이 아플 때 어떻게 하셨어요?

3. 저는 사귄 지 6개월 된 여자 친구가 있습니다. 지금 여자 친구는 매우 여자답고 조용한 성격이고, 남자들한테 인기가 많습니다. 여자 친구 초등학교 남자 동창이 한 명 있는데 제 여친하고 정말 친합니다. 둘은 같은 대학에 다녀서 수업도 같이 듣고 점심도 같이 먹고, 밤늦게까지 같이 공부할 때도 많고요. 저는 많이 신경이 쓰이는데(to be bothered) 여친한테는 이 얘기를 못 하고 있습니다. 남녀가 그냥 친구로 지낼 수 있습니까?

4. 3년 사귄 남자 친구가 있어요. 서로 사랑했고 많이 믿었죠. 그런데 말도 안 되는 일이 생겼어요. 크리스마스 약속을 하려고 여러 번 전화했는데 핸드폰이 꺼져 있었어요. 결국은 크리스마스를 혼자 보냈어요. 그리고 일주일이 지나서 남친한테 문자가 왔어요. "미안해… 우리 이제 그만 만나자." 다른 여자가 좋아졌대요. 저는 너무 놀라서 화를 낼 수도 없었어요. 이 남자 놓치고 싶지 않은데 연락도 안 되네요.

라… 다음 주제에 대해 이야기해 봅시다.

1. 한국의 연애 문화 중 '커플링' '커플티' '백일기념' 등에 대해 들어 보신 적이 있습니까? 한국의 연애 문화에 대해 더 알아보고 여러분 나라의 연애 문화와 어떻게 다른지 이야기해 봅시다.

2. 여러분은 예전 여자 친구나 남자 친구하고 친구로 지낼 수 있습니까?

3. 여러분은 친구의 예전 남자 친구나 여자 친구하고 사귈 수 있습니까?

읽기

20대~30대 미혼 남녀 데이트 보고서

결혼 정보 회사에서 8월 14일부터 21일까지 전국 미혼 남녀 561명 (남 257명, 여 304명)을 **대상으로**[GU3.9] '연인과의 데이트'를 주제로 설문 조사를 실시한 **결과,**[GU3.10] 젊은 연인들은 주로 토요일에 맛집에서 브런치 데이트를 즐기는 것으로 나타났다. 미혼 남녀의 데이트 횟수 는 평균 '주 1.9회', 데이트 준비 시간은 '53.3분', 데이트 1회 비용은 '55,900원'으로 조사됐다.

연인과 만나는 주간 데이트 횟수의 **경우,**[GU3.11] 남성은 '1회'(61.1%) '2 회'(26.1%) '3회'(6.2%), 여성은 '2회'(46.4%) '1회'(28.3%) '3회'(20.4%) 순으로 나타났다.

애인과 함께 하고 싶은 데이트 선호 요일은 남녀 모두 '토요일'(남 85.2%, 여 51%)이 압도적으로 많았다. 이어 남성은 '일요일'(6.2%) '금 요일'(4.7%), 여성은 '금요일'(22.7%) '일요일'(14.1%) 순으로 답했다.

미혼 single; unmarried 보고서 report 결혼 정보 회사 marriage agency 대상 subject 연인 one's lover; two lovers 실시하다 to conduct 횟수 number of times 평균 average 주 ~회 ~times a week 조사되다 to be investigated 주간 weekly 순으로 in order 나타나다 to appear 선호 preference 모두 all together 애인 lover (less formal than 연인) 압도적으로 overwhelmingly 이어 following 답하다 to answer

데이트 시간의 경우, 전체 응답자의 40.5%가 낮 12시 전에 만나는 것을 가장 선호한다고 답했다. 남녀**별로**[GU3.12] 구분하면 남성은 저녁(51.4%), 여성은 브런치 타임(42.4%)을 최고의 데이트 시간으로 가장 많이 선택했다.

데이트하러 나가기 위해 준비하는 데에 쓰는 시간은 남성 39.6분, 여성 64.9분으로 집계됐다. 시간은 남성 '30분 이상~1시간 미만'(44.7%), 여성 '1시간 이상~1시간 30분'(67.8%)이 가장 높았다.

미혼 남녀가 즐겨 찾는 데이트 장소는 맛집(38.3%), 영화관(27.5%), 쇼핑몰(12.3%), 카페(8.9%) 등의 순으로 나타났다.

한 번 만날 때 데이트 비용은 평균 55,900원이다. '5만 원 이상~7만 원 미만'(38%) '3만 원 이상~5만 원 미만'(32.8%) '7만 원 이상~9만 원 미만'(19.4%) 순으로 나타났다. 비용 분담은 '번갈아 가면서 낸다'(47.2%) '남성이 주로 낸다'(34.6%) '데이트 통장을 이용한다'(13.7%) 등의 순으로 답했다.

결혼 정보 회사 매니저는 "연인과의 데이트 방식에 정답은 없다. 연애를 하면서 타인하고 비교하지 말고 서로가 중심이 될 수 있는 둘만의 데이트 스타일을 만들**기를 바란다**[GU3.13]"고 말했다.

[출처: 중앙일보 '2030 미혼남녀 데이트 보고서']

전체 the whole 응답자 respondent 구분하다 to distinguish 집계되다 to be summed up 이상 over; and more than 미만 less than; below 비용 cost 번갈아 alternately; in turn 분담 share 통장 bankbook, bank account 방식 way; means 정답 right answer 타인 other people 중심 center

이해 문제

가... 다음 내용이 본문의 내용과 같으면 ○, 다르면 X에 표시하세요.

1. 이 설문은 결혼한 사람들의 연애 스타일을 조사한 것이다.　　○　　X

2. 미혼 남녀들은 일주일에 평균 1.9회 만난다고 나타났다.　　○　　X

3. 데이트 준비에 필요한 시간은 남자보다 여자가 많다.　　○　　X

4. 데이트 비용은 보통 남자가 낸다.　　○　　X

5. 토요일 저녁이 가장 선호하는 데이트 시간으로 꼽혔다.　　○　　X

나... 다음 질문에 대답해 보세요.

1. 본문은 무엇에 대한 설문 조사입니까?

2. 데이트하기 가장 좋은 날로 토요일이 꼽힌 이유는 무엇이라고 생각합니까?

3. 데이트 준비에 남자보다 여자가 시간이 더 걸리는 이유는 무엇이라고 생각합니까?

4. 윗글에 나온 내용을 바탕으로 여러분 문화와 어떻게 다른지 비교해 보세요.

문법과 용법

GU3.9

~을/를 대상으로
'taking (something/someone) as a (research) subject'

KBS는 대학생**을 대상으로** 졸업 후 희망 직업에 대해 조사했다.
KBS conducted a survey of college students on future jobs they want
after graduation.

교육청은 초등학교 교사**를 대상으로** 현재 수입에 대해 물어보았다.
The Education Office carried out a survey targeting elementary
school teachers on current income.

▶ This pattern is a contraction of ~을/를 대상으로 하여 'by taking something/
someone as a subject' with 하여 omitted. The noun 대상 means 'subject, object,
target', as in 연구 대상 'subject of study', and 하여 ("do" verb 하– + the connective
–여 'by, so, and then') means 'by making/taking/doing'.

GU3.10

~(으)ㄴ 결과   'as a result that …'

식사를 불규칙하게 **한 결과**, 그는 위장병으로 고생했다.
As a result of his irregular eating schedule [skipping meals],
he suffered from a stomach problem.

DNA를 분석**한 결과**, 경찰은 그 남자가 범인이라는 것을 알았다.

Based on the results of a DNA test, the police found the man to be guilty.

▶ This pattern is a contraction of ~ㄴ(은) 결과로 where ~ㄴ(은) is a past tense modifier ending, the Sino-Korean noun 결과 means 'result', and the particle 로 means 'as'. It is used to express cause and effect and is most commonly found in formal written texts.

GU3.11

~는/(으)ㄴ/(으)ㄹ 경우
'in the event/case (of), on the occasion (of)'

비가 **올 경우**, 소풍은 취소됩니다.

In the event of rain, the picnic will be canceled.

아직 수업을 등록하지 **않은 경우**, 자세한 정보는 웹사이트에서 확인해 주십시오.

If it is the case that you have not registered for this class yet,
please check the website for more details.

▶ This pattern is a contraction of ~ㄴ(은)/ㄹ(을) 경우에 'in the event/case that', with the omission of the particle 에 'in/at/on'. The Sino-Korean noun 경우 'circumstance, situation, case, occasion, instance, time' is preceded by a modifier ending with any tense—present, past, or future. 경우 can also be preceded by a possessive constructions, as in 만일의 경우 'just in case, for emergency'.

GU3.12

~별 '(classified) by'

지금부터 지역**별** 날씨를 알아보겠습니다.

Now, we will look at the weather by regions.

오늘 일정을 시간대**별**로 정리해 주세요.

Please organize today's schedule by hour.

▶ The Sino-Korean suffix –별 means 'classification, distinction'. When this suffix attaches to a classifiable noun such as 학교 'school', 대학 'college', 연령 'age', 인구 'population', 도 'province', and 나라 'country', it indicates '(classified) by the noun', as in 학교별 '(classified) by schools', etc. When this pattern functions as a modifier to a noun, the form ~별(의) is used, as in 지역별(의) 날씨 'the weather by regions' and 학교별(의) 학생 수 'student population by schools'. With the particle 로 'with', the pattern functions like an adverb, as in 선수들이 학교별로 들어왔다 'The players came in by schools'.

GU3.13

~기(를) 바라다 'wish/ hope/desire that ...'

감기가 빨리 낫**기를 바란다**.

I hope you get better from your cold soon.

모두 조용히 해 주시**기 바랍니다**.

We request that everyone please be quiet.

▶ This pattern consists of the "nominalizer" suffix –기 '-ing, to', which transforms the preceding predicate into a noun, and the main transitive verb 바라다 'wish, desire, want'. Since the –기 construction is the object of 바라다, the object particle 을/를 is required although it can be omitted. Basically, the pattern shows someone's desire or hope. It can also be used as a polite way of making a request.

활동

가... 다음 빈 칸에 가장 어울리는 단어를 고르세요.

1. 학생을 대상으로 교복에 대한 설문 조사를 _____.

   ㄱ. 차지했다   ㄴ. 뜸해졌다   ㄷ. 집중했다   ㄹ. 실시했다

2. 오늘 숙제는 한국과 미국의 생활 문화를 _____ 겁니다.

   ㄱ. 분석하는   ㄴ. 선호하는   ㄷ. 집계하는   ㄹ. 이별하는

3. 오늘 아파서 수업에 못 갔는데 수업 내용을 _____ 주세요.

   ㄱ. 나타내   ㄴ. 정리해   ㄷ. 행동해   ㄹ. 꼽아

4. 이번 숙제는 일주일 동안 매일 해야 합니다. 나중에 선생님이 잘
   _____ 할 수 있도록 날짜를 꼭 써 주세요.

   ㄱ. 비용   ㄴ. 구분   ㄷ. 분담   ㄹ. 방식

5. 학교에서 컴퓨터 도난 사건이 자주 일어나서 경찰이 _____로 했다.

   ㄱ. 조사하기   ㄴ. 설레기   ㄷ. 호감을 갖기   ㄹ. 선택하기

나... 주어진 표현을 사용하여 다음 대화를 완성하세요.

1. ~는/(으)ㄴ/(으)ㄹ 경우

   ㄱ: 내일 비가 많이 와도 캠핑을 할 건가요?

   ㄴ: 눈이 오면 취소해야겠지만 _____.

2. ~별로

ㄱ: 이번 장학금은 몇 명이 받을 거예요?

ㄴ: _____ 4명씩 받을 거예요.

3. ~기(를) 바란다

ㄱ: 한국어 반 친구들에게 바라는 것이 있다면 이야기해 보세요.

ㄴ: _____.

4. ~을/를 대상으로

ㄱ: 스트레스와 성적과의 관계에 대해서 누구한테 물어보면 좋을까요?

ㄴ: _____ 조사하면 좋을 거예요.

5. ~ㄴ(은) 결과

ㄱ: 건강하던 사람이 갑자기 왜 죽었대요?

ㄴ: _____ 암으로 죽었대요.

다... 다음은 대학생들의 연애 가치관에 대한 설문 조사입니다. 여러분들도 한 번 답해 보고 설문 결과를 서로 비교해 봅시다.

1. 현재 몇 살입니까? (만 나이) _____ 살

2. 몇 학년입니까?

ㄱ. 1학년   ㄴ. 2학년   ㄷ. 3학년   ㄹ. 4학년   ㅁ. 대학원

3. 지금까지 몇 명의 남자/여자 친구를 사귀었습니까?

ㄱ. 없다   ㄴ. 1~2명   ㄷ. 3~4명   ㄹ. 5명 이상

4. 처음 남자/여자 친구를 사귄 나이는 몇 살입니까? _____ 살

5. 남자/여자 친구를 어떻게 만났습니까? (복수 응답 가능)

　　ㄱ. 학교에서　　　　　　　　　ㄴ. 알고 지낸 사이에서 자연스럽게

　　ㄷ. 소개팅　　　　　　　　　　ㄹ. 인터넷

　　ㅁ. 기타 _____

6. 평균 교제 기간은 어떻게 됩니까?

　　ㄱ. 100일 미만　　　ㄴ. 3~6개월　　　ㄷ. 6개월~1년　　　ㄹ. 1년 이상

7. 만약 당신의 이상형이 나타나서 지금 남자/여자 친구와 헤어지고 자기랑
   사귀자고 하면 어떻게 하겠습니까?

　　ㄱ. 현재 남자/여자 친구와 헤어지고 이상형을 선택한다

　　ㄴ. 거절한다

　　ㄷ. 양다리를 걸친다

　　ㄹ. 기타 _____

8. 마음에 드는 남자/여자에게 이미 애인이 있다면 어떻게 하시겠습니까 ?

　　ㄱ. 관심 없는 척하면서 지켜본다.

　　ㄴ. 개의치 않고 접근한다

　　ㄷ. 그 애인과 사이가 나빠지도록 한다.

　　ㄹ. 포기한다

　　ㅁ. 기타 _____

9. 내가 선호하는 남자/여자 친구와의 나이 차이는?

　　ㄱ. _____살　　ㄴ. _____살 아래.　　ㄷ. 동갑이 좋다

　　ㄹ. 상관없다　　　ㅁ. 기타 _____

10. 남자/여자 친구를 사귈 때 가장 중요하다고 생각하는 것은 무엇입니까?

　ㄱ. 외모　　　　ㄴ. 스타일　　　　ㄷ. 성격　　　　ㄹ. 경제력

　ㅁ. 가족관계　　ㅂ. 학벌　　　　ㅅ. 나이

　ㅇ. 기타 _____

라... 다음은 설문 조사 정리에 필요한 단어나 표현들입니다. 이를 사용하여 다음 내용을
　　정리해 보세요.

> ~을/를 대상으로, 결과, 경우, 순으로, 나타나다, 답하다, 응답하다,
> 이어(서), 집계되다, 차지하다, ~에 대한, 실시하다, ~다고; ~냐고;
> ~자고; ~라고

놓친 그 사람, 언제 가장 생각나나요?

33%
주변 커플들을 볼 때,
결혼식 시즌이 될 때

25%
그(녀)가 행복한
연애 중인 걸 알았을 때

20%
문득 외로움이
찾아올 때

18%
다른 사람을 만나도
그 사람을 잊을 수 없을 때

4%
기타

추가 읽기

이별을 극복하기까지 기간은?

소셜 데이팅 서비스 회사가 20세 이상 미혼 남녀 739명을 대상으로 '이별 후유증과 극복 방법'을 물어본 결과, 남녀에 차이가 있었다.

'실연의 아픔을 극복하는 기간'은 남녀 모두 '한 달'이 제일 많았다. 이어 남성은 '1년 이상'(15.5%), '3개월'(14.2%), 여성은 '3개월'(18.6%), '6개월'(15.9%)이라고 답해 남성이 실연의 아픔이 더 오래가는 것으로 나타났다.

'실연 후 후유증'에 대해 남성은 '모든 것이 귀찮아 집에만 있었다'(35%)는 답변이 가장 많았고 그 뒤로 '술과 담배로 건강 악화'(27.2%)가 있었다. 그러나 '후유증이 없다'고 답한 남성도 22.1%나 됐다. 여성도 '모든 것이 귀찮아 집에만 있었다'(58%)는 대답이 가장 많았고, '더크게 웃고 씩씩하게 산다'(36.8%)는 답변이 2위를 차지해 특이했다. 그러나 남성과 달리 '후유증이 없다'고 답한 여성은 2.6%에 불과했다.

'실연 극복법'은 남녀 의견이 아주 달랐다. 남성은 '일, 학업에 집중한다'(32.5%), '취미 생활을 열심히 한다'(29.2%)고 답했고, 반면 여성은 '선물 버리기, SNS에서 연애 흔적 지우기'(52.8%)를 선택했다. 다음으로는 '주위 사람들에게 솔로 선언'(31.6%)을 하는 등, 보다 적극적으로 이별을 알리기도 했다.

[출처: 이데일리 '이별 후 얼마 동안 새로운 연애를 금지해야 할까?']

극복하다 to overcome 기간 period of time 후유증 aftereffect 실연 breakup; broken heart 오래가다 to last long 귀찮다 to be troublesome 악화 getting worse 씩씩하다 to be energetic 차지하다 to be ranked 특이하다 to be unique ~와/과 달리 unlike ~ 불과하다 to be mere, just 학업 study 집중하다 to concentrate 흔적 trace 주위 surrounding 선언 announcement 적극적 to be active

한국 영화에 나온 사랑과 연애에 대한 유명한 대사들

- "사랑이 어떻게 변하니?" – 봄날은 간다

- "사랑하기 때문에 사랑하는 것이 아니라 사랑할 수밖에 없기 때문에 당신을 사랑합니다." – 번지점프를 하다

- "전 지금 사랑에 빠졌어요. 너무 아파요. 그런데, 계속 아프고 싶어요." – 연애소설

- "인연이란 말은 시작할 때 하는 말이 아니라 모든 게 끝날 때 하는 말이에요." – 동감

- "더 사랑하는 자. 약자." – 음란서생

- "열심히 사랑했잖아, 열심히 잊었잖아. 그럼 된 거야." – 싱글즈

- "만나야 할 사람은 언젠가 꼭 만나게 된다고 들었어요." – 접속

- "너 마음에서 날 지우는 것도 배신이야." – 약속

- "사랑이 변하는 게 아니라 사람이 변하는 거야." – 너는 내 운명

- "새로운 사람은 절대 만나기 싫어. 나를 설명해야 되잖아." – 후아유

대사 lines or dialogues 번지점프 bungee jumping 동감 agreement 약자 the weak 음란 *lit.* obscene 서생 *lit.* a young student 잊다 to forget 싱글즈 singles 접속 access 배신 betrayal 변하다 to change 운명 fate; destiny 절대 absolute

■■ 번역문 ■■

CONVERSATION: Please Give Me Some Advice!

Relationship Counseling Radio Program

Counselor: Okay, next caller. Hello?

Listener: Hello. I'm a 22-year-old woman living in Seoul.

Counselor: What is your concern?

Listener: I have a boyfriend, but lately, I've been thinking that he's lost interest in me.

Counselor: Ah, so you're saying it seems like your boyfriend has changed?

Listener: Yes.

Counselor: How long have you been dating?

Listener: About 400 days…

Counselor: 400 days…so what is it about your boyfriend that's bothering you?

Listener: Um… he's a little cold. He behaves like an acquaintance rather than my boyfriend.

Counselor: You don't think there is another girl, do you?

Listener: There is no possibility something like that is happening because I meet with him almost every day.

Counselor: Then, why do you think he's acting like that?

Listener: I don't know. Last time we met, he said that his feelings toward me aren't like they used to be…and that he's trying but it's not working…

Counselor: Did your boyfriend suggest breaking up?

Listener: He didn't. But, it seems like he's waiting for me to suggest breaking up first.

Counselor: So, what did you say to your boyfriend?

Listener: I said I needed time to get my thoughts straight, and now about a month has passed. But we've had no contact.

Counselor: Despite what you heard from him, even though he hasn't even contacted you, do you still want to keep seeing him?

Listener: We have a lot of memories…we were really happy…

Counselor: Ah that's really unfortunate. My heart aches for you. But if your boy-
               friend said that, it means he doesn't have feelings for you anymore. It's
               hard to change how one feels.

Listener: But, my boyfriend still wears our couple ring and his SNS profile picture
               is still a picture with me…so that's why I think he still has feelings for
               me.

Counselor: That's probably because you haven't broken up yet. It'll probably be very
               painful, but if you keep hanging onto him it's going to be more difficult,
               and your boyfriend will despise the relationship even more.

Listener: So, then I need to think our relationship has ended and just let him go?

Counselor: You've got nothing to worry about. Right now it may seem so hard
               that you could die, but after time passes it'll all be forgotten. You're still
               young and have a lot of things to do, so hang in there. You'll meet a good
               guy!

READING:
Dating Report of Unmarried Men and Women in Their 20s and 30s

The marriage agency conducted a survey of 561 unmarried men and women (257
men, 304 women) throughout the country from August 14th to the 21st on the topic
of "couple dates". According to the results of this survey, young couples generally
prefer having a brunch date on Saturdays at good restaurants. It was also found that
unmarried people have 1.9 dates per week, that it takes them 53.3 minutes to prepare
for a date, and that a single date's cost comes to 55,900 won.

As for the number of dates couples prefer to have per week, it was found that 61.1%
of men go on one date per week, 26.1% have two dates per week, and 6.2% have three
dates per week. For women, 46.4% have two dates, 28.3% have one date, and 20.4%
have three dates.

For both men (85.2%) and women (51%) the response was overwhelmingly in favor of Saturdays as the day they prefer to spend with their significant other with 6.2% of men answering Sunday, and 4.7% answering Friday. Whereas, (for the same question) for women, 22.7% answered Friday, and 14.1% answered Sunday.

As for the time of day to have a date, 40.5% answered that meeting before 12 was most preferred. "Brunch time" was reported as the most preferred time by all respondents. Looking at the responses from men and women separately, a majority of men (51.4%) selected dinner/evening, and many women (42.4%) chose brunch time.

In terms of the time it takes to prepare for a date, on average men require 39.6 minutes, while women need 64.9 minutes. A large proportion of men (44.7%) spend at least 30 minutes and at the most one hour preparing, and a majority of women (67.8%) spend between one hour and an hour and a half.

As for the date locations enjoyed by unmarried men and women, answers included nice restaurants (38.3%), the movie theater (27.5%), shopping malls (12.3%), cafes (8.9%), and nearby attractions (8.6%).

On average respondents spend 55,900 won over the course of a single date. It was found that 38% of respondents spend between 50,000 and 70,000 won, 32.8% spend between 30,000 and 50,000 won, and 19.4% spend between 70,000 and 90,000 won. As for the method used to determine who pays for a date, answers included "taking turns paying" (47.2%), "the man usually pays" (34.6%), and that they are "using a date bankbook" (13.7%).

A wedding agency manager said "there's no right answer when it comes to dating methods. Rather than comparing with others when dating, we hope that people will create a dating style just for themselves, one that allows the focus to be on each other."

[Source: JoongAng Daily, 2030 Unmarried Men and Women Dating Report]

FURTHER READING:
How Long Does It Take to Get over a Breakup?

A social dating service company asked 739 unmarried men and women over the age of 20 about the aftereffects of breaking up and methods for getting over breakups. The results showed a difference between men and women.

As for the length of time it takes to get over a broken heart, both men (36.3%) and women (34.2%) responded with "one month" more than any other answer. Following this, 15.5% of men said "more than one year", and 14.2% answered within "three months". As for women, 18.6% answered "three months", and 15.9% said "six months". These results show that men feel the pain of a broken heart longer than women.

When asked about the aftereffects of a breakup, the most common answer given by men (35%) was that they "stay at home because everything bothers them". This answer was followed by "decline in health due to alcohol and smoking" (27.2%). However, 22.1% reported having no aftereffects. Women also reported "staying at home because everything bothers them" as the aftereffect of a breakup with 58% giving this as their answer. Interestingly, the second-place answer (36.8%) was "laughing louder and living vigorously". However, in contrast to men, only 2.6% of women reported having no breakup aftereffects.

As for methods for overcoming a breakup, men and women had major differences in opinion. For men, 32.5% stated that they "focus on work or studying", and 29.2% answered by saying that they "enthusiastically pursue a hobby". Meanwhile, 52.8% of women responded by saying that they "throw away presents and clean up traces of their relationship on SNS accounts". This answer was followed by 31.6% of women "announce their single status to people around them at work, school, etc.", demonstrating that women more actively let people know about their breakup.

CULTURE:
Famous Lines on Love and Romance from Korean Movies

- "How can love change?"– One Fine Spring Day
- "I love you, not because I am simply in love with you, but because I can't help but love you." – Bungee Jumping of Their Own
- "I've fallen in love now. It hurts so much, but I want to keep on hurting." – Lover's Concerto
- "Fate is not what you say when you start a relationship, but what you say when everything is over." – Ditto
- "The one who loves more is the weaker of the two."– Forbidden Quest
- "You loved him so much, and you tried so hard to forget him. So that's that." – Singles
- "I heard that you will someday meet, the person whom you were meant to meet." – The Connection
- "It is also betrayal to erase me from your heart." – A Promise
- "It is not the love that changes, but people that change." – You Are My Sunshine
- "I definitely don't want to meet someone new. Because then I'd have to explain myself." – School 2015

▌▌ 단어 ▌▌

간접 화법	indirect quotation	불과하다	to be mere, just
결혼 정보 회사	marriage agency	비교하다	to compare
고민	worry, concern	비용	cost
구분하다	to distinguish	상담	counsel
귀찮다	to be troublesome	상담자	counselor
극복하다	to overcome	서생	a young student
기간	period of time	선언	announcement
나타나다	to appear	선호	preference
노력하다	to try hard	설문 조사	survey
놓아 주다	to let go	순으로	in order
답하다	to answer	실시하다	to conduct
대사	lines or dialogues	실연	breakup; broken heart
대상	subject	싱글즈	singles
동감	agreement	씩씩하다	to be energetic
마음(을) 정리하다	to clear one's mind	악화	getting worse
		안타깝다	to be sorry; to be pitiful
마음이 무겁다	to have a heavy heart	압도적으로	overwhelmingly
마음이 식다	to lose interest in someone	애인	lover (less formal than 연인)
매달리다	to cling to; to beg	약자	the weak
모두	all together	연애	date
미만	less than; below	연인	one's lover; two lovers
미혼	single; unmarried	예전	the past
방식	way; means	오래가다	to last long
번갈아	alternately; in turn	~와/과 달리	unlike ~
번지점프	bungee jumping	운명	fate; destiny
변하다	to change into	음란	obscene
보고서	report	응답자	respondent
분담	share	이상	over; and more than
분석하다	to analyze	이어	following

인연	affinity; fate	차갑다	(one's attitude) to be cold
잊다	to forget		
잊혀지다	to be forgotten	차지하다	to be ranked
적극적	to be active	청취자	(radio) listener
적절하게	appropriately, properly	추억	recollection, reminiscence
전체	the whole		
절대	absolute	커플링	matching rings between lovers
젊다	to be young, youthful		
젊은이	young people	타인	other people
접속	access	통장	bankbook, bank account
정답	right answer	특이하다	to be unique
조사되다	to be investigated	평균	average
주 ~회	~ times a week	학업	study
주간	weekly	행동하다	to behave
주위	surrounding	헤어지다	to break up
중심	center	횟수	number of times
집계되다	to be summed up	후유증	aftereffect
집중하다	to concentrate	흔적	trace

4과 지역별 관광지와 특산물

Lesson 4 Tour Sites and Regional Products

학습 목표

내용
- 자신의 경험이나 생각을 말할 때 필요한 표현을 배운다.
- 인터넷에서 한국어로 된 관광 정보를 검색할 수 있도록 한다.

문화
- 한국의 관광지와 명소를 알아본다.
- 한국의 지리를 익히고 지역별 특산물을 살펴본다.

전주 한옥마을

부산 국제시장

지역별 by locations 관광지 tourist sites 특산물 regional products 경험 experience
정보 information 명소 famous places 지리 geography 익히다 to master

■ 생각해 봅시다

가 ˮ 다음에 대해 같이 이야기해 봅시다.

1. 여러분 나라의 유명한 도시나 관광지는 어떤 곳들이 있습니까?

2. 여러분들이 알고 있는 한국의 도시나 관광지는 어떤 곳들이 있습니까?

3. 한국에서 가 본 곳이나 가 보고 싶은 관광지에 대해 이야기해 봅시다.

4. 한국에서 여행해 본 곳들의 특산물로는 어떤 것들이 있습니까?

5. 다음은 한국의 지도입니다. 여러분이 가 본 곳이나 가 보고 싶은
   곳을 표시해 보세요.

강원도에 가요

대학 휴게실에서

지윤: 이제 곧 여름 방학인데 뭐 **할 계획이야**^{GU4.1}?

린다: 글쎄요, 선배. 이번 방학에는 아직 **한 번도**^{GU4.2} 간 적이 없는
        곳에 가 보고 싶어요. 어디가 좋을까요?

지윤: 그동안 한국에서 어디에 가 봤어?

린다: 지난 겨울 방학에는 전주 한옥마을에 갔었고 5월 연휴에는
        부산에 가 봤어요. 부산에서 영화 '국제시장'에서 나온 국제
        시장에도 갔어요. 이번 방학에는 **웬만하면**^{GU4.3} 산도 있고 바
        다도 있는 곳에 가 보고 싶어요.

지윤: 그럼 혹시 강원도에 가 봤어?

린다: 아니요. 작년 여름에 **갈까 했었는데**^{GU4.4} 잘 몰라서 안 갔어요.

지윤: 그럼 강원도에 가 봐. 강원도 설악산에 가면 산과 바다 다 볼
        수 있어.

린다: 그런데 설악산까지 교통이 불편하지 않아요?

지윤: 아니, 이제는 고속도로가 잘 돼 있어서 교통이 아주 편리해.
        서울에서 고속버스를 타고 가면 두 시간도 안 걸려. 그리고
        가는 김에^{GU4.5} 바닷가에 있는 낙산사에 꼭 가 봐. 거기에 홍련

휴게실 lounge 선배 upper classmate 한옥마을 village of Korean houses 연휴 long
weekend 국제 international 웬만하면 if possible – 곳 place 설악산 Seorak Mountain
낙산사 Naksan Temple 홍련암 Hongnyeon (*lit.* Small) Temple

암이 있거든.

린다: 어디요? 홍련암이요? 어떤 곳인데요?

지윤: 홍련암은 작은 절인데 절 바닥에 있는 구멍으로 바다가 보여.

린다: 신기하네요! 꼭 가 봐야겠어요. 그럼, 설악산에는 뭐가 있어요?

지윤: 흔들바위가 유명해. 흔들바위는 큰 바위인데 밀면 흔들리지만 떨어지지는 않거든.

린다: 정말요? 그런 게 있어요?

지윤: 그리고 설악산에서 케이블카를 타고 산에 올라가면 경치가 아주 멋있어.

린다: 그렇군요. 참, 그런데 강원도 먹거리는 뭐가 있나요?

지윤: 음… 춘천 닭갈비, 횡성 한우 뭐 이런 것들이 유명한데, 설악산이 있는 속초에서는 생선회를 꼭 먹어 봐야지. 특히 신선한 오징어 회가 유명해.

린다: 아… 작년에 갔**어야 했는데**[GU4.6] 아쉽네요. 저는 회를 정말 좋아하거든요.

지윤: 아 참, 정동진도 꼭 가 봐. 한국에서 가장 일찍 해돋이를 볼 수 있는 곳 중 하나라서 사람들이 새해에 많이 가거든. 여름에는 물론 바닷가에서 수영도 즐길 수 있고.

린다: 고마워요, 선배. **생각보다**[GU4.7] 볼거리가 많네요. 선배 **덕분에**[GU4.8] 좋은 정보를 얻었어요. 이번 여름 방학에는 3박 4일 정도로 강원도 여행 계획을 세워 볼게요.

절 Buddhist temple 바닥 floor 구멍 hole 바위 rock 밀다 to push 흔들리다 to be shaken
떨어지다 to fall, drop 경치 scenery 닭갈비 spicy stir-fried chicken 한우 Korean beef
신선하다 to be fresh 생선회 raw fish, sashimi 아쉽다 to feel sorry, regret 해돋이 sunrise
새해 the New Year 볼거리 things to see

이해 문제

가... 다음 내용이 대화의 내용과 같으면 ○, 다르면 X에 표시하세요.

    1. 린다는 설악산에 가 본 적이 있다.   ○   X

    2. 서울에서 설악산까지 교통은 좀 불편하다.   ○   X

    3. 설악산은 바다에서 가깝다.   ○   X

    4. 강원도는 해산물이 유명하다.   ○   X

    5. 많은 사람들이 새해에 정동진에 간다.   ○   X

나... 다음 질문에 대답해 보세요.

    1. 지윤과 린다는 어떤 관계인가요?

    2. 린다가 지금까지 한국에서 가 본 곳은 어디입니까?

    3. 이 글에서 소개한 강원도 관광지는 어떤 곳이 있습니까?

    4. 홍련암은 어떤 곳입니까?

    5. 흔들바위는 어떤 것입니까?

    6. 정동진은 어떤 곳입니까?

문법과 용법

GU4.1

~(으)ㄹ 생각/계획/예정/작정이다
'think/plan/intend/intend'

이번 주말에 빨래를 **할 생각**이에요.

I'm thinking of doing laundry this weekend.

여름 방학에 한국에 **갈 계획**이에요.

I am planning to go to Korea this summer vacation.

올해는 꼭 담배를 끊을 **작정**이에요.

I made up my mind definitely to quit smoking this year.

언제 졸업**할 예정**이에요?

When do you plan to graduate?

▶ This pattern is used to talk about future plans or intentions. It is composed of the prospective (or future) modifier ending –(으)ㄹ followed by the Sino-Korean noun 생각 'thinking', 계획 'planning', 예정 'planning', or 작정 'intention' and the copula 이다 'is'.

GU4.2

한 번도/하나도 + negative construction
'not even once/not at all'

나는 한국에 가 본 적이 **한 번도** 없어.

I have never been to Korea.

우리 수업은 **하나도** 재미가 없어.

Our class is not fun whatsoever.

어제 술을 많이 마셔서 **하나도** 기억이 안 나네.

I drank so much yesterday, so I don't remember a single thing.

▶ In Korean, there are a large number of words that can only be used with
predicates in negative form, as in 다시는 '(never) again' in '**다시는** 거짓말하지
않을게요 'I will never tell a lie'. These words are often called "negative polarity
items". 한 번도 and 하나도 are such negative polarity items. Other items include
밖에 'except for', 별로 '(not) particularly', 조금도 '(not) at all', 전혀 '(not) at all',
and 좀처럼 'seldom'.

GU4.3

웬만하면   'if possible, if you do not mind, if tolerable';
가능하면   'if possible'

웬만하면 집에 가서 쉬세요.

If possible, please go home and rest.

가능하면 짧게 통화해 주세요.

Please, make the call as brief as possible

▶ 가능하다 means 'to be possible, feasible', while 웬만하다 means 'to be not very bad, tolerable, fairly good'. 가능하면 'if possible' and 웬만하면 'if you do not mind; if you could arrange it; if tolerable, if possible' are often used interchangeably in the same contexts, although the meanings are slightly different.

GU4.4

~(으)ㄹ까 하다   'think of doing, intend to do'

A. 여기는 어떻게 오셨어요?

What brought you here?

B. 커피나 한 잔 마**실까 하**고요.

I was just thinking of having a cup of coffee.

저는 다음 학기에 한국 문화 수업을 **들을까 생각하**고 있어요.

I am thinking of taking Korean culture class next semester.

▶ This pattern combines the indirect question ending –(으)ㄹ까 'whether (I) will' and the verb 하다 'do, think, say'. The subject of the indirect clause is usually the speaker. 하다 may be replaced with verbs of thinking such as 생각하다 'think', as in 오전 중에 돌아올까 해요/생각해요 'I expect to come back before noon'.

GU4.5

~는/(으)ㄴ 김에
'while one is at/about it; on the occasion that'

샤워하**는 김에** 욕실도 청소 좀 해.

Since you're already taking a shower, perhaps you could also clean
the bathroom.

말이 나**온 김에** 언제 파티 할지 결정하자.

Since we're talking about it, let's decide when we are going to have a party.

▶ This pattern is composed of the modifier ending ~는 (present) or ~(으)ㄴ
(past), followed by the bound noun 김 'occasion, chance' and the particle
에 'at/in/on'. It is used to express that while one is doing something, he/she
takes the opportunity to do something else. Instead of a verb, a noun can precede 김에, as in 우리는 술김에 싸웠어요 'We fought due to the alcohol'.

GU4.6

~었/았어야 하다   one should have done ~

지하철 2호선을 **탔어야 했**는데 실수로 3호선을 타서 약속에 늦었어요.

I should have taken line number 2, but I got on line number 3 by mistake so
I was late for my appointment.

이번 시험은 공부를 열심히 **했어야 했**는데.

I should have studied harder for this test.

▶ This pattern expresses the speaker's regret of not doing something that should have been done. It consists of the past tense suffix –었/았 + the particle 어야 'only if it be, indeed' + the verb 하다 'do'. ~어야 하다 means '(one) must/ should (do)'. With the preceding past suffix, it means '(one) should/must have done'. In using this pattern, the past form of the verb 하다 is usually used, as in 나는 집에 있었어야 했다 'I should have stayed home; I had to stay at home'.

GU4.7

생각보다 + adjective/adverb
'compared to what I thought'

생각보다 영화가 **재미없**네.

This movie is more boring than I thought it would be.

한국어 수업이 **생각보다 어려워**요.

Korean class is harder than I expected.

▶ This pattern is composed of the Sino-Korean noun 생각 'thinking, thought' followed by the "comparative" particle 보다 'than'. As is the case in all comparative constructions, this pattern is required to be followed only by an adjective or adverb in the main clause.

~ 덕분에   'thanks to, since'

N 덕분에 Thanks to N ...

> 감사합니다. 선생님 **덕분에** 한국어를 잘 하게 됐어요.
>
> Thank you. Thanks to you, my teacher, I can now speak Korean well.

V (으)ㄴ/는 덕분에

> 일찍 출발한 **덕분에** 약속 시간에 안 늦었어요.
>
> Since I got going early, I was not late for my appointment.
>
> 저는 매일 운동하는 **덕분에** 건강을 유지할 수 있어요.
>
> Since I exercise every day, I can stay healthy.

▶ This pattern is used to indicate a reason that causes a positive result. It consists of the Sino-Korean noun 덕분 'indebtedness' and the particle 에. It can be translated into "thanks to". Since 덕분 is a noun, it can be preceded either by a (possessive) noun, as in 선생님(의) 덕분에, or by a relative clause, as in 운동하는 덕분에. This pattern is comparable to N 때문에 and V기 때문에, which expresses a reason in a neutral or somewhat negative way.

활동

가... 다음 밑줄 친 곳에 적당한 표현을 고르세요.

1. 이번 추석 _____은/는 일주일이나 되니까 여행 좀 가야겠어요.

   ㄱ. 연휴   ㄴ. 계획   ㄷ. 방학   ㄹ. 주말

2. 보통은 학교까지 차로 30분이면 충분한데 요즘 공사 때문에 1시간 _____
   걸려요.

   ㄱ. 별   ㄴ. 정도   ㄷ. 만   ㄹ. 보다

3. 이 식당은 주인이 직접 키우는 채소로 요리하기 때문에 재료가 아주
   _____.

   ㄱ. 바빠요   ㄴ. 편리해요   ㄷ. 신선해요   ㄹ. 신기해요

4. 아르바이트를 아직 구하지 못했어요. 그래서 요즘 돈이 _____.

   ㄱ. 많아요   ㄴ. 아쉬워요   ㄷ. 웬만해요   ㄹ. 흔들려요

5. 난기류(turbulence)로 비행기가 _____ 수 있으니 안전벨트를 매 주시기
   바랍니다.

   ㄱ. 키울   ㄴ. 밀   ㄷ. 흔들릴   ㄹ. 올라갈

나... 다음 질문에 주어진 표현을 사용하여 대화를 완성해 보세요.

1. ~ㄹ/을 생각/계획/예정/작정이다

   ㄱ: 이번 여름 방학에 뭐 할 거예요?

   ㄴ: _____.

2. 한 번도

ㄱ: 김치 만들어 본 적 있어요?

ㄴ: _____.

3. 웬만하면/가능하면

ㄱ: 이번 학기에 아르바이트 해요?

ㄴ: _____.

4. ~(으)ㄹ까 하다

ㄱ: 오늘 일요일인데 뭐 할까요?

ㄴ: _____.

5. ~ㄴ/은/는 김에

ㄱ: 어디 가세요?

ㄴ: 김치 좀 사려고 한국 마켓에 가요. 왜요?

ㄷ: _____.

6. ~ㅆ/았/었어야 하다

ㄱ: 한국어 학기 말 시험 잘 봤어요?

ㄴ: 아니요. _____.

7. 생각보다

ㄱ: 지난 학기 한국어 수업 어땠어요?

ㄴ: _____.

8. 덕분에

ㄱ: 한국에 여행 잘 다녀오셨어요?

ㄴ: 네, _____.

다... 대화 내용에 맞게 보기에 주어진 장소를 관련된 내용과 연결하세요.

1. 전주 _____

2. 부산 _____

3. 설악산 _____

4. 춘천 _____

5. 정동진 _____

ㄱ. 국제시장

ㄴ. 닭갈비

ㄷ. 한옥마을

ㄹ. 흔들바위

ㅁ. 해돋이

라... 다음은 강원도 여행 일정표입니다. 질문에 대한 답을 인터넷에서 찾아 여행 계획을 세워 보세요.

〈양양·속초·춘천 관광 일정〉

08:00 서울 용산역 출발 → 10:20 양양 낙산사 도착

동해의 푸른 절 낙산사 관람

11:00 낙산사 출발 → 11:20 설악산 도착

설악산 관람 | 권금성 케이블카 관광

12:00 설악산 출발 → 12:30 점심 장소 도착

점심 식사: 속초 오징어 회 + 매운탕

13:30 출발 → 15:00 춘천 남이섬 도착

문화와 예술의 섬! 남이섬

17:00   **저녁 식사: 닭갈비 + 막국수**

---

1. 설악산 케이블카 탑승료는 얼마입니까?

2. 춘천역에서 용산역까지 가는 교통비는 얼마입니까?

3. 남이섬 입장료는 얼마인가요?

4. 닭갈비와 함께 먹을 음식은 무엇입니까?

5. 이 과의 대화에 나온 장소를 포함하여 여행 계획을 만들어 보세요.

읽기

지형과 지역별 특산물

한국은 동·서·남 삼면이 바다인 반도이다. 해안이 길기 때문에 해안을 따라 도시들이 발달했고 인천, 부산 같은 큰 항구 도시들이 있다. 삼면의 바다 중 동해는 바다가 깊고 물이 깨끗해서 유명한 해수욕장이 많다. 서해는 바다 색깔이 누렇고 탁해서 황해라고도 부른다. 바다가 얕고 해산물이 많이 난다. 그리고 남해는 섬이 많고 경치가 아름다워서 관광객들이 많이 찾는다. 한국에는 3천 개가 넘는 **크고 작은** ^{GU4.9} 섬들이 있다.

한국에는 또 산이 많다. 국토의 약 **4분의 3**^{GU4.10}이 산인데 특히 동쪽에 산이 많다. 한반도에서 제일 높은 산은 백두산(2,750미터)인데 백두산은 북한에 있다. 남한에서는 제주도의 한라산이 1,950미터로 제일 높고, 그 다음 전라도의 지리산(1,915미터)과 강원도의 설악산(1,708미터) 순으로 높다. 한라산, 지리산, 설악산은 모두 국립공원이고 여름에는 도시보다 시원해서 피서지로 인기이다.

지형 geographical features 삼면 three sides 반도 peninsula 해안 coast 항구 harbor, port 발달하다 to develop 동해 the East Sea 해수욕장 beach 누렇다 to be (golden) yellow 탁하다 to be murky 서해 the Yellow Sea (=황해) 얕다 to be shallow 넘다 to be more or over 섬 island 국토 country, territory 4분의 3 three-fourths 북한 North Korea 남한 South Korea 국립공원 national park 피서지 summer resort

　　지역별로 다양한 특산물들이 있는데, 먼저 경기도는 쌀이 유명하고 맛있는 쌀과 맑은 물로 만든 막걸리도 인기가 있다. 충청북도는 인삼과 도라지가 많이 생산되고, 충청남도에서는 한국 음식에서 빠질 수 없는 마늘을 많이 키운다.

　　전라북도에서는 나물이 많이 나고, 전라남도는 미역, 젓갈, 굴비와 같은 해산물과 크고 맛있는 배가 옛날부터 생산되어 왔다. 경상북도의 특산물로는 사과가 있고, 경상남도는 여러 종류의 해산물과 곶감으로 유명하다. 그리고 남한에서 가장 북쪽에 위치한 강원도는 감자와 옥수수가 많이 자라고, 또한 목장이 많아서 소고기와 우유, 치즈 등 유제품도 많이 생산된다. **마지막으로**^{GU4.11} 가장 남쪽에 위치한 제주도는 따뜻해서 귤이 많이 재배된다. 이처럼 지역**마다**^{GU4.12} 날씨와 지형**에 따라**^{GU4.13} 생산되는 특산물도 다르다. 한국에서 여행할 때 이런 특산물들을 즐겨 보면 더욱 의미 있는 여행이 될 것이다.

인삼 *insam* (ginseng) 도라지 balloon flower root 나물 wild greens 미역 sea mustard
젓갈 salted seafood 굴비 partly dried yellow corvina fish 배 pear 생산되다 to be
produced 곶감 dried persimmon 위치하다 to be located 감자 potato 옥수수 corn
목장 ranch 유제품 dairy products 귤 mandarin orange 재배되다 to be cultivated
자라다 to grow (up), be raised

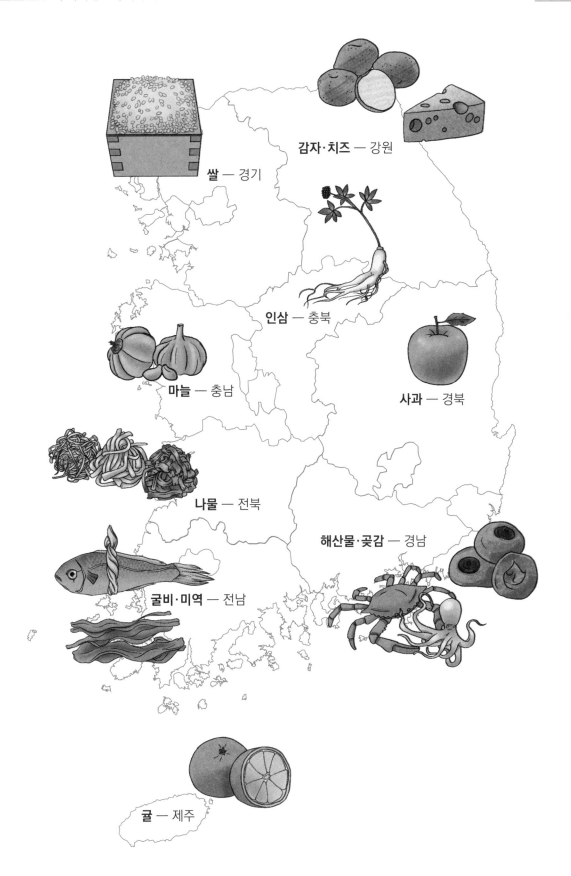

쌀 — 경기

감자·치즈 — 강원

인삼 — 충북

마늘 — 충남

사과 — 경북

나물 — 전북

해산물·곶감 — 경남

굴비·미역 — 전남

귤 — 제주

이해 문제

가... 다음 내용이 본문의 내용과 같으면 ○, 다르면 X에 표시하세요.

1. 한국은 섬이 많은 섬나라이다.   ○   X

2. 한국에는 큰 항구 도시들이 있다.   ○   X

3. 전라남도와 경상남도는 해산물이 유명하다.   ○   X

4. 강원도는 한국에서 가장 남쪽에 있다.   ○   X

5. 제주도는 한국에서 가장 따뜻한 지역이다.   ○   X

나... 다음 질문에 대답해 보세요.

1. 반도란 무엇입니까?

2. 한라산, 설악산, 지리산이 피서지로 유명한 이유는 무엇입니까?

3. 한국은 삼면이 바다라서 어떤 것들이 발달해 있습니까?

4. 동해, 서해, 남해는 서로 어떤 차이가 있습니까?

5. 지역별로 생산되는 특산물을 정리해 봅시다.

강원도: 경기도:

경상남도: 경상북도:

전라남도: 전라북도:

충청남도: 충청북도:

제주도:

문법과 용법

Adj 1 고 Adj 2 'adjective and adjective'

이 지역에는 **높고 낮**은 산들이 많습니다.

There are many tall and short mountains in this area.

이 공원에는 **크고 작**은 동물들이 살고 있습니다.

There are animals of various sizes living in this park.

길고 짧은 것은 대 봐야 안다.

Don't judge the differences by their appearances.

(*lit*. We don't know if it is too long or too short until we measure it.)

▶ Some pairs of adjectives that have contrastive meanings are used in this pattern to describe variations of a certain state. Other examples include 쓰고 달다 'be bitter and sweet', and 많고 적다 'be many and few'.

▶ When adjectives of similar meanings are used in this way, they emphasize the common connotations of them. Examples are 맵고 짠 음식 meaning 'spicy and salty food', 춥고 배고프다 meaning 'to be cold and hungry', and 착하고 예쁘다 meaning 'to be nice and pretty'.

GU4.10

numeral Y + 분의 + numeral X
'numeral X -ordinalized numeral Y(s)'

한 시간의 **4분의 1**은 15분이다.

A quarter of an hour is fifteen minutes.

나는 숙제의 **3분의 2**를 끝냈어.

I have finished two-thirds of my homework.

▶ Fractions in Korean are expressed by the formula "the denominator + 분 'fractions/portions' + 의 'of' + the numerator". Note that ~분의 is read [~부네]. Thus, '5-hundreds' is expressed by 100분의 5.

1/4 = 4분의 1 [사분에 일] 'one-fourth; one-quarter' (*lit.* Out of 4 parts, there is 1.)

1/2 = 2분의 1 [이분에 일] 'one-half; a half' (*lit.* Out of 2 parts, there is 1.)

▶ For mixed fractions, the whole number is read first, followed by 와/과 'and' before reading the fraction:

1 1/4 = 1과 4분의 1 'one and one-quarter'

2 2/3 = 2와 3분의 2 'two and two-thirds'

GU4.11

마지막으로 'lastly, finally, in conclusion'

서울에 갔을 때 오전에는 박물관을 두 곳 구경하고, 오후에는 한국 요리 강습을 받았어요. 그리고 **마지막으로** 저녁에 쇼핑을 했어요.

When I went to Seoul I visited two museums in the morning, and then in the afternoon I had a Korean cooking class. And lastly, in the evening I went shopping.

제가 윤 교수님을 **마지막으로** 뵈었을 때가 작년이었어요.

The last time I met Professor Yoon was last year.

▶ 마지막으로 is an appropriate conjunctive expression to use when introducing the last point or a conclusion, as in the first sentence above. Additionally, the expression 마지막으로 can be used as an adverbial clause meaning the last time something occurred/was done as in the second sentence above.

GÜ4.12

~마다 'each, every'

명절 풍습은 집집**마다** 조금씩 차이가 있다.

Holiday traditions are slightly different among families.

우리 아버지는 날**마다** 등산을 하러 산에 가신다.

My father goes to the mountains to hike every day.

연말이 되니 거리**마다** 바쁘게 오고 가는 사람들이 많아졌다.

Since it is the end of a year, there has been an increase in busy people walking around every street.

▶ The particle of frequency ~마다 is added to a noun (including a bound noun) to add the meaning 'each' or 'every'. Examples with a bound noun include 가는 곳**마다** 나는 환영을 받았어 'I was warmly welcomed everywhere I went', and 내가 집에 전화를 할 때**마다** 아무도 전화를 받지 않았어요 'Every time I called home, nobody answered'.

GU4.13

~에 따라(서) 'depending on ~, following ~'

학생들은 성적**에 따라** 반이 정해졌습니다.

Students were put into different classes based on their grades.

이번 주말 계획은 상황**에 따라서** 바뀔 수 있습니다.

The plan for this weekend can change depending on what happens.

▶ 따르다 means 'to follow'. The meaning of N에 따라서 is 'by following N' or 'depending on N'. On the other hand, the expression ~에 따르면 means 'according to ~'.

활동

가... 다음 밑줄 친 곳에 어울리는 단어를 고르세요.

1. 나는 여행을 하면 항상 그 지역의 _____을/를 사 가지고 온다.

   ㄱ. 특산물   ㄴ. 경치   ㄷ. 물가   ㄹ. 재료

2. 부산, 요코하마, 뉴욕, 시애틀 등은 항구가 _____ 도시이다.

   ㄱ. 발달한   ㄴ. 깊은   ㄷ. 짓는   ㄹ. 탁한

3. 아이오와는 옥수수가 많이 _____는 곳이다.

   ㄱ. 유명하   ㄴ. 생산되   ㄷ. 다양하   ㄹ. 위치하

4. 여름에 더위를 피하기 가장 좋은 _____은/는 집이라고 생각한다.

   ㄱ. 반도   ㄴ. 국토   ㄷ. 바다   ㄹ. 피서지

5. 하와이에서는 파인애플을 _____한다.

   ㄱ. 발달   ㄴ. 여행   ㄷ. 위치   ㄹ. 재배

나... 숫자를 포함하여 다음 문단을 읽어 보세요.

우리 반 학생은 모두 40명입니다. 40명 중에서 1/5은 외국에서 온 학생이고 그중에서 1/4은 일본 사람입니다. 그리고 우리 반에서 2/3는 남학생입니다. 전공을 보면 가장 인기 있는 전공은 컴퓨터 공학인데 우리 반 1/2의 학생이 컴퓨터를 전공하고 있습니다.

다... 보기에서 적당한 표현을 찾아 문장을 완성하세요.

> 곳, ~마다, 마지막으로, 분의, ~에 따라서

1. 저는 건강을 위해 날 _____ 요가를 합니다.

2. 날씨 _____ 옷을 다르게 입어요.

3. 다음 방학 때 가장 여행하고 싶은 _____은 어디예요?

4. 오늘 발표에서는 제가 역사에 대해 말씀드렸습니다.

   _____ 질문이 있으면 해 주세요.

5. 의사 선생님이 약을 반만 먹으라고 하셨어요. 그러니까 원래 먹던 거보다

   2 _____ 1만 먹어야 되는 거네요.

라... 다음 설명에 맞는 지역의 이름을 찾아 쓰고 그 지역의 특산물을 더 알아보세요.

(ㄱ) 경기도	(ㄴ) 경상남도	(ㄷ) 경상북도
(ㄹ) 전라북도	(ㅁ) 제주도	(ㅂ) 충청북도

A. _____

이천 쌀이 인기이다.

B. _____

인삼과 도라지가 유명한데
한약 재료로도 쓰인다.

D. _____

사과가 유명하다.

C. _____

나물이 많이 난다.

E. _____

가장 남쪽에 위치해
따뜻해서 귤이 생산된다.

한국의 사투리

한국에서는 모든 지역에서 공통적으로 사용되는 말을 표준어라고 하는데, 표준어는 서울에서 쓰는 말을 기준으로 정한 것이다. 표준어 이외에 특정 지방에서만 쓰는 말을 사투리라고 하는데 한국의 사투리로는 경상도, 전라도, 충청도, 강원도, 제주도 등의 사투리를 들 수 있다. 사투리마다 독특한 억양이 있고 쓰는 단어가 다른 경우도 있지만 한국의 사투리들은 서로 차이가 아주 크지는 않아서 지역 사람들끼리 의사소통을 하는 데에 큰 문제는 없다. 하지만 한국어를 배우는 사람들이 사투리를 이해하기는 쉽지 않을 수도 있다. 여기서는 경상도, 전라도, 충청도 사투리에 대해서 간단히 알아보자.

경상도 사투리

경상도 사투리는 억양의 높낮이가 심하다. 그리고 경상도에서는 "ㅆ" 발음을 "ㅅ"처럼 해서 "쌀"을 [살]처럼 발음하기도 한다. 또 "ㅡ" 발음을 "ㅓ"처럼 해서 "증거"를 [정거]처럼 발음한다. 그리고 "ㅕ"를 "ㅔ"처럼 발음해서 "형님"을 [헹님]처럼 발음한다. 표준어와 다른 표현으로는 "맞나?"(그래? 진짜?), "와?"(왜?) 등이 있다. 또 질문을 할 때에는 문장 끝에 "~노?" 또는 "~나?"를 쓰는데 예를 들면 "뭐하노?"(뭐하니?), "밥 먹었나?"(밥 먹었니?)처럼 말한다. 즉, "~노?"는 내용을 물을 때, 그리고 "~나?"는 "네" 혹은 "아니요"로 답할 수 있는 질문에 사용한다.

사투리 local dialect　공통적 common　표준어 standard language　기준 standard; criteria
이외에 besides (this)　특정 specifics　독특하다 to be unique　억양 intonation　의사소통
communication　간단히 briefly　높낮이 high and low, rise and fall　증거 proof, evidence

전라도 사투리

전라도 사투리는 억양의 높낮이는 심하지 않지만 모음이 표준어와 다르게 나타나는 경우가 많다. 예를 들어 전라도에서는 "아닌디"(아닌데), "그라쟤"(그렇지), "넘어져 브렀다"(넘어져 버렸다), "괴기"(고기), "그짓말"(거짓말), "그라믄"(그러면)처럼 말한다. 그리고 문장 끝에 "~잉"을 붙여 "그래요, 잉"(그렇죠)처럼 말하기도 한다. 표준어와 다르게 쓰는 표현들로는 "겁나게"(정말로) "시방"(지금) "쪼께"(조금) "으짜쓰까?"(어떻게 할까?) 등이 있다.

충청도 사투리

충청도 사람들은 다른 지방의 사람들보다 좀 느리게 말하는 편이다. 문장 끝의 "~요"를 "~유"에 가깝게 말한다. 예를 들어 "몰라유"(몰라요), "됐슈"(됐어요, 괜찮아요) 등이 있다. 질문할 때에는 "~여?" "~겨"를 문장 끝에 쓰는데 "뭐여?"(뭐야?), "어디 가는 겨?"(어디 가는 거야?)처럼 이야기한다. 그리고 "~해"를 "~햐" 또는 "~혀"로 발음해서 "뭐 혀?"(뭐 해?), "공부 참 잘 햐"(공부 참 잘 해)처럼 말을 한다. 표준어와 다른 표현들로는 "기다"(맞다)와 경상도에서도 쓰는 "댕기다"(다니다) 등이 있다.

지방을 여행하면 각 지역의 특색 있는 사투리가 실제로 사용되는 것을 들을 수 있다. 그러나 요즘은 교통의 발달과 텔레비전 등의 영향으로 젊은 세대들은 사투리를 예전보다 적게 쓰는 편이다. 특히 제주도 사투리는 알아 듣기 힘들기로 유명하지만 요즘 젊은 사람들은 거의 안 쓴다고 한다. 사투리가 적게 쓰여서 의사소통은 더 편해졌지만 각 지방의 고유한 특징이 없어져서 아쉬워하는 사람들도 많이 있다.

모음 vowel 문장 sentence 지방 regions except Seoul and its vicinity 실제 actual 세대 generation 고유 indigenous 아쉬워하다 to feel the lack of

한국의 유명한 지역 축제

	축제 이름	할 수 있는 활동들
1월	**화천 산천어 축제** Whacheon Sancheoneo Ice Festival	얼음 낚시, 썰매 타기, 눈 조각 구경
2월	**보성 차 밭 빛 축제** Boseong Tea Plantation Light Festival	차 밭 구경하기, 차 마시기
3월	**제주 들불 축제** Jeju Fire Festival	제주도 전통 음식 체험, 제주도 문화 배우기
4월	**진해 군항제** Jinhae Cherry Blossom Festival	벚꽃 구경, 각종 공연 관람
5월	**고양 국제 꽃 박람회** Goyang International Flower Festival	세계의 여러 가지 꽃 관람
6월	**강릉 단오제** Gangneung Danoje Festival	단오절에 대해 배우기, 한국의 민속놀이 체험

얼음 ice 낚시 fishing 조각 sculpture 차 밭 tea plantation 체험 experience 벚꽃 cherry blossoms 각종 various kinds 공연 performance 관람 viewing 단오절 Korean traditional holiday that falls on the 5th day of the 5th lunar month 민속놀이 folk games

	축제 이름	할 수 있는 활동들
7월	**보령 머드 축제** Boryeong Mud Festival	머드 마사지, 대천 해수욕장에서 해수욕
8월	**이천 국제 조각 심포지엄** International Sculpture Symposium Icheon	조각 관람, 작가 워크숍, 작가 강연
9월	**평창 효석 문화제** Hyoseok Cultural Festival	이효석의 대표작 '메밀꽃 필 무렵'의 배경이 된 메밀꽃 밭 둘러보기
10월	**부산 국제 영화제** Busan International Film Festival	세계의 영화 관람
11월	**서울 빛초롱 축제** Seoul Lantern Festival	아름다운 등으로 장식된 거리에서 걷기
12월	**정동진 해돋이 축제** Jeongdongjin Sunrise Festival	새해 해돋이 보기

해수욕 sea bathing 조각 sculpture 대표작 major work 메밀 buckwheat 무렵 about the time 둘러보다 to look around 등 lantern 장식되다 to be decorated

■■ 번역문 ■■

CONVERSATION: Let's Go to Gangwon Province

Chiyun: Linda, it's almost summer vacation now. What are your plans (for summer break)?

Linda: I'm not sure, *sŏnbae* (*lit.* senior, address term used for someone who entered school or work before the speaker, explained further in chapter six). During the break, I want to go somewhere I haven't visited yet. Where would be a good place to go to?

Chiyun: While you've been here, where have you been to in Korea?

Linda: Last winter break, I went to the Jeonju Hanok Village, and during the long weekend in May, I went to Busan. In Busan, I even went to International Market, the market that was featured in the movie '*Kukje Sijang*', 'Ode to My Father'. This break, I want to go somewhere with both mountains and the ocean, if possible.

Chiyun: Then have you by chance, been to Gangwon Province?

Linda: No, I was going to go last summer, but I didn't because I did not know much about it.

Chiyun: Then try going to Gangwon Province. If you go to Seorak Mountain in Gangwon Province, you can see both mountains and the ocean.

Linda: Isn't the traffic to Seorak Mountain bad (*lit.* inconvenient) though?

Chiyun: No, now that the highway is set up well, getting there is very convenient. If you take an express bus, it takes less than two hours to get there. And on your way, make sure to go to Naksan Temple which is on the beach. That's where Hongnyeonam is.

Linda: Where? Hongnyeonam? What kind of place is that?

Chiyun: Hongnyeonam is a small temple, and the sea can be seen from a hole in the floor of the temple.

Linda: That's amazing! I should really go see it. Then, what's there in Seorak Mountain?

Chiyun: The Hŭndŭl-bawi (*lit.* a rocking boulder) is famous. Hŭndŭl-bawi is a boulder that if you push, it will rock but doesn't fall.

Linda: Really? There is such a thing?

Chiyun: And if you take the cable car up at Seorak Mountain, the view is really awesome.

Linda: I see. Oh, but what is good to eat in Gangwon Province?

Chiyun: Hmm… well things like *Chuncheon takalbi* (chicken ribs), and *Hoengseong hanu* (Korean beef) are famous. And in Sokcho, where Seorak Mountain is, you have to try slices of fresh raw fish. The fresh raw squid is especially famous.

Linda: Woo… I should have gone last year. It's too bad. I love raw fish.

Chiyun: Oh, by the way, you should go to Jeongdongjin, too. It is the place where you can see the sunrise first (*lit.* the earliest) in Korea, so a lot of people go there for New Year's Eve. And of course, you can enjoy swimming at the beach in the summer, too.

Linda: Thank you, *sŏnbae*. There are more things to see than I had expected. Thanks to you, *sŏnbae*, I have a lot of good information. This summer break, I'll make travel plans to go to Gangwon Province for about three nights and four days.

READING: Geographic Characteristics and Regional Products

Korea is a peninsula with the sea on three sides to the East, West, and South. Because the coast is long, cities have developed along the coast, and there are large port cities like Incheon and Busan. Of the three seas, the East Sea is deepest, and there are many famous beach destinations because the water is so clear. The West Sea is also called the Yellow Sea due to the fact that it is yellowish in color and is murky. The sea is shallow and much seafood is produced. Additionally, there are many islands in the South Sea and because the scenery is so beautiful, it attracts many tourists. There are over 3,000 small and large islands in Korea.

There are also many mountains in Korea. About three-fourths of Korea is mountainous region, and there are especially many mountains in the east. The tallest mountain on the Korean Peninsula is Mt. Baekdu (2,750 meters), which is located in North Korea. In South Korea, Mt. Halla in Jeju Island is the tallest at 1,950 meters, followed by Jeolla Province's Mt. Jiri (1,915 meters) and Gangwon Province's Mt. Seorak (1,708 meters). Halla, Seorak, and Jiri Mountains are all national parks, and during the summer they are popular summer resorts for escaping the heat because the mountains are cooler than the cities.

There are various specialty products by region. First, Gyeonggi Province is famous for rice, and *makkŏlli* is also popular, which is made with delicious rice and clear water. Chungcheongbuk Province produces a lot of herbal root *insam* or ginseng and bellflower roots, and Chungcheongnam Province grows much garlic, which cannot be left out in Korean food.

In Jeollabuk Province, many wild greens are produced, and ever since olden times, Jeollanam Province has produced seafood such as seaweed, salted fish, yellow corvina, as well as large delicious pears. Gyeongsangbuk Province's famous regional products include apples, and Gyeongsangnam Province is known for a variety of seafood and dried persimmons. Additionally, Gangwon Province, which is located in the most northern part of South Korea, grows a lot of potatoes and corn. Furthermore, there are many ranches and farms, producing much beef and dairy products, such as milk and cheese. Lastly, on Jeju Island, which is located at the southernmost tip of Korea, many tangerines are harvested because it is warm there. As such, each region has its own local products, depending on its weather and terrain. If one tries enjoying these local products when traveling in Korea, the trip will become a much more meaningful one.

FURTHER READING: The Dialects of Korea

In Korea, the speech commonly used in all regions is called the standard language. The standard language is based on the language used in Seoul. Speech styles other than the standard language, which are used in specific regions are called *sat'uri*, or dialects. The Korean dialects include those of the Provinces of Gyeongsang, Jeolla, Chungcheong, Gangwon, Jeju, etc. Each dialect has a unique accent, and sometimes the words are also different. However, the Korean dialects do not significantly differ from each other, so there is no major problem in communicating with people of different regions. Nevertheless, comprehending the dialects may not be easy for (non-native) learners of the Korean language. Here, we will briefly examine Gyeong-sang, Jeolla, and Chungcheong dialects.

Gyeongsang Dialect

The Gyeongsang dialect has many intonational fluctuations. (The standard Korean expressions are given in parenthesis.) In Gyeongsang Province, the sound of "ㅆ" is pronounced like "ㅅ," so the word 'rice,' "*ssal* (쌀)" is pronounced like 'flesh,' [sal (살)]. Also the (vowel) sound "ŭ (ㅡ)" is pronounced like "ŏ [ㅓ]," with *chŭnggŏ* 증거 (meaning 'proof') being pronounced like [*chŏnggŏ* 정거] (which means stopping). Additionally, "yŏ (ㅕ)" is pronounced like "e [ㅔ]," so "*hyŏngnim* (형님)," (an honorific word for an older brother) is pronounced [heng-nim, 헹님]. With regards to expressions that differ from the standard language, there is "*manna* (맞나)?" (meaning "Is it correct?"), "*kŭrae? chintcha* (그래? 진짜?)?" (for 'oh?' or 'really?'); and "wa [와]?" for "*wae* (왜)," (which means 'why?'), etc. Additionally, when asking questions, people use "~ *no*, 노?" or "~ *na* 나?" at the end of their sentences. For example, they say "mwo ha-no?" 뭐 하노?" (*mwo ha-ni?*, 뭐하니?) (to ask what one is doing). Also, they say "pam mŏgŏn-na?, 밥 먹었나?"(*pam mŏgŏn-ni?*, 밥 먹었니?). Thus "~*no*?" is used when asking about content, and "~*na*?" when asking yes-no questions.

Jeolla Dialect

The intonation fluctuation of the Jeolla Province dialect is not very significant, but vowels often appear differently from the standard language. For example in Jeolla Province, the following [in brackets] are how people say the vowels. [anindi, 아닌디] (*aninde*, 아닌데 or it is not), [kŭrajyae, 그라쟤] (*kŭrŏch'i*, 그렇지 or right), [nŏmŏjyŏ-bŭrŏtta, 넘어져 브렀다] (*nŏmŏjyŏ-bŏryŏtta*, 넘어져 버렸다 or ended up falling), [koegi, 꾀기] (*kogi*, 고기 or meat), [kŭjinmal, 그짓말] (*kŏjinmal*, 거짓말 or a lie), [kŭramŭn, 그라믄] (*kŭrŏmyŏn*, 그러면 or then). Also at the end of sentences, they add "*ying*, 잉" as in "*kŭraeyo, ing* 그래요, 잉" instead of *gŭrŏch'yo* (그렇죠). The expressions that are different from standard language include "*kŏmnage* 겁나게" for the standard *chŏngmallo* (정말로 meaning truly), "*shibang*, 시방" for *chigŭm*, (지금 or now), "*tchokke*, 쪼께" for *chogŭm* (조금 or a little), "*ŭtchyassŭkka?* 으짜쓰까?" for *ŏttŏk'e halkka?* (어떻게 할까? or how should one do it)?

Chungcheong Dialect

People who use Chungcheong dialect tend to talk more slowly than the people who use the dialect of other regions. Also, they pronounce the sentence ending "~yo" closer to "~yu". For example are "*molla-yu* 몰라유" (*molla-yo* 몰라요 or don't know), "*twaets-yu* 됐슈" (*twaessŏ-yo kwaench'ana-yo* 됐어요, 괜찮아요 it is alright), etc. When asking a question, they use "~*yŏ*, ~여?" and "*kyŏ* ~겨?" at the end of sentences as in "*mwŏyŏ?*, 뭐여?" (*mwŏya* 뭐야? or what is it?) "*eŏdi kanŭn kyŏ?*, 어디 가는 겨?"(*ŏdi kanŭn kŏya* 어디 가는 거야? or where are you going?). Expressions that differ from the standard language include "*taenggida*, 댕기다 (*tanida* 다니다, to go on regular basis), etc. which is also used in Gyeongsang Province.

When traveling to the different regions, one can easily hear the actual use of the distinct dialects of each region. However, with the development of transportation and the influence of television recently, younger generations tend to use dialect less than before. In particular, though the Jeju Island dialect is known for its incomprehensibility, young people apparently hardly use the dialect these days. This decrease in the use of regional dialects has made communication easier; however, there are many who feel sorry because the unique characteristics of each region disappeared.

CULTURE: Famous Local Festivals in Korea

Month	Festival	Activities
January	Whacheon Sancheoneo Ice Festival	Ice fishing, sledding, seeing ice sculptures
February	Boseong Tea Plantation Light Festival	Seeing tea plantation, tea tasting
March	Jeju Fire Festival	Experiencing traditional Jeju Province, learning the culture of Jeju Province
April	Jinhae Cherry Blossom Festival	Seeing cherry blossoms, watching various performances
May	Goyang International Flower Festival	Seeing various flowers from around the world
June	Gangneung Danoje Festival	Learning about the (traditional) Dano holiday, experiencing traditional Korean folk games
July	Boryeong Mud Festival	Mud massage, swimming at the Daecheon Beach
August	International Sculpture Symposium Icheon	Seeing sculptures, artist workshops, artist lectures
September	Hyoseok Cultural Festival	Visiting the buckwheat flower field which was the setting of Hyoseok Lee's major work, "When the Buckwheat Flowers Bloom"
October	Busan International Film Festival	Watching films from around the world
November	Seoul Lantern Festival	Strolling the streets decorated with beautiful lanterns
December	Jeongdongjin Sunrise Festival	Watching the New Year's sunrise

▪▪ 단어 ▪▪

각종	various kinds	단오절	Korean traditional holiday that falls on the 5th day of the 5th lunar month
간단히	briefly		
감자	potato		
경치	scenery		
경험	experience	닭갈비	spicy stir-fried chicken
고유	indigenous	대표작	major work
곳	place	도라지	balloon flower root
공연	performance	독특하다	to be unique
공통적	common	동해	the East Sea
곶감	dried persimmon	둘러보다	to look around
관광지	tourist sites	등	lantern
관람	viewing	떨어지다	to fall, drop
구멍	hole	메밀	buckwheat
국립공원	national park	명소	famous places
국제	international	모음	vowel
국토	country, territory	목장	ranch
굴비	partly dried yellow corvina fish	무렵	about the time
		문장	sentence
귤	mandarin orange	미역	sea mustard
기준	standard; criteria	민속놀이	folk games
나물	wild greens	밀다	to push
낙산사	Naksan Temple	바닥	floor
낚시	fishing	바위	rock
남한	South Korea	반도	peninsula
넘다	to be more or over	발달하다	to develop
높낮이	high and low, rise and fall	배	pear
		벚꽃	cherry blossoms
누렇다	to be (golden) yellow	볼거리	things to see
		북한	North Korea
		4분의 3	three-fourths

사투리	local dialect	젓갈	salted seafood
삼면	three sides	정보	information
새해	the New Year	조각	sculpture
생산되다	to be produced	조각가	sculptor
생선회	raw fish, sashimi	증거	proof, evidence
서해	the Yellow Sea (=황해)	지리	geography
선배	upper classmate	지방	regions except Seoul
설악산	Seorak Mountain		and its vicinity
섬	island	지역별	by locations
세대	generation	지형	geographical features
실제	actual	차 밭	tea plantation
아쉬워하다	to feel the lack of	체험	experience
아쉽다	to feel sorry, regret	탁하다	to be murky
얕다	to be shallow	특산물	regional products
억양	intonation	특정	specific
얼음	ice	표준어	standard language
연휴	long weekend	피서지	summer resort
옥수수	corn	한옥마을	village of Korean
웬만하면	if possible		houses
위치하다	to be located	한우	Korean beef
유제품	dairy products	항구	harbor, port
의사소통	communication	해돋이	sunrise
이외에	besides	해수욕	sea bathing
익히다	to master	해수욕장	beach
인삼	*insam* (ginseng)	해안	coast
자라다	to grow	홍련암	Hongnyeon
장식되다	to be decorated		(*lit.* Small) Temple
재배하다	to cultivate	휴게실	lounge
절	Buddhist temple	흔들리다	to be shaken

한류

Lesson 5 *Hallyu*, Korean Wave

학습 목표

내용 • 대중문화와 관련된 표현을 배운다.

• 의견을 표시할 때 사용하는 표현을 익힌다.

문화 • 한류의 배경과 역사를 이해한다.

• 한류의 영향을 알아본다.

대중 public; mass 상대방 the other (party) 영향 influence

■ 생각해 봅시다

가 ▸▸ 다음 질문에 대해 함께 이야기해 봅시다.

   1. 한국의 대중문화인 '한류'에 대해 아는 것을 말해 보세요.

   2. 요즘 인기 있는 한국의 영화, 드라마, 노래, 연예인 등에 대해서
      말해 보세요.

   3. 여러분이 좋아하는 한국의 영화, 드라마, 노래, 연예인 등에 대해서
      이야기해 보세요.

   4. 여러분이 관심을 가지고 있는 한국의 음식, 패션, 게임 등이 있으면
      토론해 보세요.

나 ▸▸ 한국 대중문화가 인기 있는 나라는 어디가 있을까요? 그 이유는
      무엇이라고 생각합니까?

다 ▸▸ 여러분 나라에도 알려져 있는 한국의 연예인이나 노래, 드라마는
      어떤 것이 있습니까?

연예인 entertainer 토론 discussion, debate 이유 reason

대화

한류와 한국 수업

수업 시작 전 교실에서

지윤: 너 요즘 한국 드라마 보니?

샌디: 아니, 한국 드라마는 한번 보기 **시작하면**^{GU5.1} 그만둘 수 없어서 방학하면 보려고 해.

민준: 샌디가 한국 드라마를 볼 거라고 **생각도 못 했는데**^{GU5.2}...

샌디: 내 **말이**^{GU5.3}... **나야말로**^{GU5.4} 한국 드라마**는커녕**^{GU5.5} 한국 아이돌 팬이 될 거라고는 전혀 생각도 못 했지.

마크: 그래서 나는 드라마 말고 영화를 많이 봐. 역사 영화를 좋아하는데 '태극기 휘날리며'하고 '국제시장'을 보면서 한국전쟁에 대해서 더 알게 됐어.

지윤: 어머! 역사 안 어려워?

마크: 아니, 너도 봐 봐. 난 다음 학기에 한국 역사 수업 들을 거야.

민준: 한국 현대 문화 수업에서는 아이돌 그룹 이야기가 나온다던데.

샌디: 정말? 정말? 나, 한국 아이돌 팬이거든. 춤 정말 잘 추잖아! 미국에서 하는 공연에 많이 갔었어.

그만두다 to stop, quit 전혀 (not) at all 태극기 휘날리며 the movie "Taegukgi, Brotherhood of War" (*lit.* Fluttering the Korean Flag) 한국전쟁 Korean War 아이돌 teen idol 공연 performance

민준: 아이돌 그룹이 데뷔 전에 훈련 받는 얘기도 나오고 한류가 외
      국에서 인기가 있는 이유도 배우는 것 같아.

마크: 그러고 보니 한류의 범위가 꽤 넓네. 영화, 드라마, K-pop은
      물론이고^{GU5.6} 음식, 패션까지 포함하잖아. 게다가 온라인 게
      임, 비디오 게임들도 세계적으로 아주 유명하고.

민준: 그렇네. 한류의 경제적 효과도 클 거야. 드라마나 영화 촬영
      지에 관광객도 많이 방문하고 연예인이 광고하는 상품도 잘
      팔린대. 연예인들이 쓰는 물건도 잘 팔리고.

샌디: 맞아. N서울타워는 드라마 촬영으로 더 유명해졌거든. 작년
      에 갔다 왔는데 외국인 관광객들이 많이 왔었어.

지윤: 다음 학기에 우리 한국 문화 수업 같이 듣는 건 어때?

민준: 당연하지!

샌디: 나도 좋아. 너희들이 듣는다면 나도 **안 들을 수가 없지.**^{GU5.7}

마크: 난 역사 수업을 들을 건데, 한국 문화 수업은 다른 수업하고
      시간이 겹치지 않으면 들을게.

훈련 training 범위 scope, range 포함하다 to include 효과 effect 촬영지 filming site 상품
products 촬영하다 to film 당연하지! Of course! 너희들 you (guys) 겹치다 to overlap,
double

이해 문제

가... 본문을 읽고 다음 내용이 대화의 내용과 같으면 ○, 다르면 X에 표시하세요.

1. 한국 현대 문화 수업에서 영화와 한국 역사에 대해 배울 수 있다.　　○　　X

2. 샌디는 한국 영화를 자주 보고 게임을 많이 한다.　　○　　X

3. 한국 역사 수업 내용에는 한류의 경제적 효과도 포함된다.　　○　　X

4. 온라인 게임과 비디오 게임은 세계의 여러 나라에서 인기가 있다.　　○　　X

5. 마크는 다음 학기에 친구들과 함께 한국 문화 수업을　　○　　X
   듣고 싶어 하지 않는다.

나... 대화를 읽고 다음 질문에 답하세요.

1. 샌디가 요즘 한국 드라마를 안 보는 이유는 무엇입니까?

2. 한류의 범위에는 어떤 것이 있습니까?

3. 한류가 가져다주는 경제적 효과는 무엇이 있습니까?

4. N서울타워에는 왜 관광객이 많이 있었습니까?

5. 샌디, 지윤, 민준은 다음 학기에 어느 수업을 같이 들을 겁니까?

문법과 용법

GU5.1

~기 시작하다 'begin, start'

저는 대학에서 한국어를 공부하**기 시작했**어요.

I started learning Korean in college.

한국어가 점점 어려워지**기 시작했**어요.

Korean has little by little begun to get difficult.

▶ As a transitive verb, 시작하다 'begin, start' requires an object. If the object is a noun, the object particle follows the noun, as in 나는 등산을 시작했다 'I began hiking'. If the object is a clause, the nominalizer suffix –기 is attached to the predicate of the clause, as in 미아는 노래하기 시작했다. No past or future tense marking is allowed before –기.

GU5.2

~다고/라고 생각하다 'I think that …'

저는 민준 씨가 정말 노래를 잘 한**다고 생각해**요.

I think that Minjun sings really well.

저는 한국 사람들이 부지런하**다고 생각해**요.

I think that Korean people are diligent.

저는 제니퍼가 좋은 학생이**라고 생각해**요.
I think that Jennifer is a good student.

▶ The indirect quotation form can be used to express one's own thoughts or beliefs. Depending on the situation, you can use verbs that express your mental actions such as 생각하다 'think', 믿다 'believe', 여기다 'consider', or 짐작하다 'guess' in the main clause.

▶ An expanded structure ~(으)ㄹ 거라고 생각도 못 하다 is used to express one's disbelief about something or someone that one did not think of, or is beyond one's expectations or imagination, as in 오늘 비가 올 거라고 생각도 못 했어요 'I never thought that it would rain today'.

GU5.3

내 말이 Expressing agreement: 'That's what I mean'

내 말이 (그 말이야)./제 말이 그 말이에요. That's what I mean.

그러게 (말이에요)./그러게요. You can say that again.

그러니까 (말이에요)./그러니까요. You can say that again.

누가 아니래(요). Tell me about it.

맞아(요). That's correct.

정말 그래(요). Indeed!

▶ It is polite to express your agreement when you have conversations. Above expressions can be used when you want to say that you are agreeing with the person you are talking with.

GU5.4

N(이)야말로   'It is the very N that..., indeed'

이 책이야말로 대학생들이 꼭 읽어야 하는 책입니다.

This book is the very book college students must read.

너야말로 이 문제에 책임이 있는 사람이야.

It is you, indeed, who is responsible for this problem.

▶ This pattern is used when you want to emphasize the referent of the noun or pronoun (N) as the exact thing you want to talk about. The particle (이)야말로 is composed of the particle (이)야 'only if it be, indeed' and 말로 'in words', literally meaning 'talking only (if it is) about'.

GU5.5

~은/는커녕   'let alone ...'

아침**은커녕** 물도 한 잔 못 마셨어.

I couldn't drink even a cup of water, let alone eat breakfast.

여행**은커녕** 주말에도 일을 해야 해요.

Forget going on a trip; I have to work even on the weekend.

▶ This pattern is used to indicate that something is far less possible than something else in the following phrase. The particle 은/는커녕 consists of the topic particle 은/는 and the particle 커녕 'anything but, far from'. The following contrasted phrase usually takes the particle 도 'even'.

> **GU5.6**
>
> ## ~은/는 물론(이고) 'not to mention, to say nothing of'

제니는 영어**는 물론** 한국어도 잘 해요.

Not to mention English, Jenny also speaks Korean well.

우리 교수님은 학식**은 물론이시고** 경험도 많으시다.

Not to mention being knowledgeable, our professor also has a lot of experience.

▶ When the Sino-Korean noun 물론 (*lit.* 'not to discuss') 'a matter of course' combines with the copula (이), it means 'it is a matter of course, it goes without saying', as in 제니가 영어를 잘 하는 것은 물론이에요 'It goes without saying that Jenny speaks English well'. When 물론이– combines with the connective –고 'and', it functions as a connective with the meaning 'not to mention'. In this case, 이고 can be omitted without changing the meaning.

▶ When 물론 is used as an adverb, it has a meaning of 'of course':

　　가: 저 좀 도와주시겠어요? Can you help me?
　　나: **물론** 도와 드려야지요. Of course, I will help you.

GU5.7

[negation] ~(으)ㄹ 수가 없다
'be compelled/forced/obliged to; have to; must'

컴퓨터 공학이 전공이라서 김 교수님 수업을 **안 들을 수 없**다.

As my major is computer science, I have to take Professor Kim's courses.

부모님이 학비를 보내 주시니까 나는 열심히 공부하**지 않을 수 없**다.

Since my parents pay my tuition I am obliged to study hard.

▶ Negation is expressed in two ways, in short and long forms. Short form negation is expressed by placing a negative adverb before the verb or adjective, as in 안 간다 and 안 크다. Long form negation is expressed by a verb or adjective + –지 않다, as in 가지 않는다 and 크지 않다. Both forms of negation occur before ~(으)ㄹ 수가 없다, as observed in the above example sentences.

▶ The pattern [negation] ~(으)ㄹ 수 없다 (*lit.* 'there is no way not to do/be') is used to indicate that a certain situation or event has forced the subject of the sentence to do something or to be in such a state. The pattern contains two negative forms, but it does not express any negative meaning. The usage of this pattern is somewhat similar to that of the pattern ~지 않으면 안 된다 'should'.

활동

가... 밑줄 친 부분에 적당한 말을 고르세요.

1. N서울타워는 드라마를 _____해서 유명해졌다.

   ㄱ. 촬영   ㄴ. 방문   ㄷ. 포함   ㄹ. 공연

2. 한류는 드라마나 K-pop만 있는 것이 아니라 그 범위가 _____ 넓다.

   ㄱ. 게다가   ㄴ. 꽤   ㄷ. 잘   ㄹ. 당연히

3. 저는 K-pop을 좋아해서 아이돌 그룹의 _____에 많이 갔었어요.

   ㄱ. 공연   ㄴ. 훈련   ㄷ. 광고   ㄹ. 관광지

4. 제 인생에 가장 큰 _____을/를 끼친 사람은 고등학교 때 선생님입니다.

   ㄱ. 관심   ㄴ. 고백   ㄷ. 영향   ㄹ. 이유

5. 좋은 _____은/는 상품을 잘 팔리게 한다.

   ㄱ. 과정   ㄴ. 광고   ㄷ. 범위   ㄹ. 공연

나... 보기에 주어진 표현을 골라 문장을 완성하세요.

~기 시작하다	~은/는커녕	~은/는 물론이고
~(이)야말로	~다고/라고 생각하다	~지 않을 수가 없다

1. ㄱ: 보통 하루에 몇 시간 게임 해요?

   ㄴ: 저는 한번 _____면 3시간은 해야 돼요.

2. ㄱ: 혹시 한국어 반에 있는 리사 씨 알아요?

    ㄴ: 그럼요. 리사 씨는 한국어 _____, 중국어도 잘 해요.

3. ㄱ: 열심히 공부하는데도 한국어 듣기를 잘 못 하겠어. 넌 어때?

    ㄴ: 난 듣기 _____, 단어도 자꾸 잊어버려.

4. ㄱ: 준기라는 학생에 대해 어떻게 생각하세요?

    ㄴ: 저는 준기 씨가 좋은 학생 _____.

5. ㄱ: 음악 소리 좀 작게 해 줄래?

    ㄴ: 너 _____ 책 읽을 때 소리 내지 마!

6. ㄱ: 왜 아르바이트를 하세요?

    ㄴ: 여행을 하고 싶은데 돈이 없어서 _____.

다... 본문의 내용에 따라 관련 있는 단어들을 연결한 후 그 표현을 사용하여 예문을 만들어 보세요.

1. 경제적 •	• 겹치다
2. 관심이 •	• 생기다
3. 시간이 •	• 얻다
4. 세계적으로 •	• 유명하다
5. 인기를 •	• 효과

라... 대화를 바탕으로 다음 질문에 대해 생각해 봅시다.

1. 한국 드라마는 한번 보기 시작하면 그만둘 수 없다고 많이들 말합니다.
   즉, '중독성(addiction)'이 있다는 것인데, 그 이유를 말해 보세요.

2. 여러분이 한국어를 공부하는 이유에 한류가 포함됩니까?
   여러분 친구 중에 한류의 영향으로 한국어를 공부하는 학생이 있습니까?

한류의 성장과 배경

'한류(韓流)'란 한국의 문화가 해외에서 유행하는 현상을 말한다. 일반적으로 한류는 1990년대 중반 드라마로 아시아에서 시작되었다고 **본다.**[GU5.8] 이렇게 드라마로 시작된 한류는 1990년대 말 댄스 그룹 '클론'과 'H.O.T.' 등이 중국에서 인기를 얻게 되면서 분야를 넓혀 나갔고 아시아 전체를 대상으로 '동방신기' 같은 그룹이 만들어졌다. 그후, 춤으로 유명한 가수들이 두각을 나타내는데 2002년에 '비', 2003년에는 '보아'가 일본에서 큰 인기를 얻었다. 이어서 2004년에는 가수 **겸**[GU5.9] 배우 '장나라'가 중국에서 인기를 얻었고 2007년에는 힙합 그룹 '빅뱅'이 일본에서 성공했다. 또한 2009년부터는 '원더걸스' '소녀시대' 등의 걸그룹이 해외에서 인기를 끌기 시작했다. 아이돌 스타의 성공에는 팬클럽과 SM, YG, JYP 같은 한국 엔터테인먼트 회사들이 큰 역할을 했다.

한류는 아시아를 넘어 미국에서도 인기를 얻었는데 2012년 싸이의 '강남스타일'은 미국 빌보드 100 차트의 2위까지 오르고 유튜브에서 30억 건에 가까운 조회 수를 기록했다. 더 나아가 남자 그룹 '방탄

성장 growth 해외 overseas 현상 phenomenon 1990년대 1990s 중반 the middle phase
분야 area, field 전체 the whole 두각을 나타내다 to distinguish oneself 성공하다 to be
successful 역할을 하다 to play a role 조회 수 number of views or searches 더 나아가
furthermore

소년단(BTS)'도 2017년에 그들의 노래를 미국 빌보트 차트에 올리는 등 한류를 지속시켜 나갔다.

드라마 역시 인기가 계속되어 2000년 '가을동화'가 동남아시아에서 인기가 있었고, 2004년 '겨울연가'는 일본 NHK TV에서 방송되어 큰 인기를 얻게 되었다. 같은 해 한국 음식을 주제로 한 역사극 '대장금'이 아시아는 물론 미국과 중동, 그리고 아프리카의 약 90개국에서 방송되어 큰 인기를 얻었다. '대장금'의 영향으로 비빔밥과 김치 같은 한식이 세계 널리 알려졌으며 이제는 외국의 퓨전 요리에 한국 고추장이나 김치를 사용하는 것을 흔히 볼 수 있다.

영화 역시 한류에서 중요한 부분이다. 2000년대 초반 '엽기적인 그녀'("My Sassy Girl"), '태극기 휘날리며'("Taegukgi, The Brotherhood of Love"), '쉬리'("Shiri") 등이 한류 열풍을 더했다. 또 임권택 감독의 '서편제'("Sopyonje") 등의 한국 영화가 세계적으로 유명한 칸, 베니스, 베를린 국제영화제에서 감독상을 받았다.

한국의 게임도 세계적으로 인기가 높은데 그 수출액이 K-pop의 11배나 될 정도로 큰 규모이다. 1970년대 중반 비디오 게임으로 시작된 한국 게임은 처음에는 다른 나라의 게임을 따라하는 수준이었다. 그러다가 1980년대 말부터 '신검의 전설'(The Legend of Sword) 등의 한국산 게임이 나오기 시작했고 점점 더 종류도 많아졌다. 이어 스타크래프트 챔피언 임요환 등 프로게이머도 많이 등장했으며 컴퓨터

동남아시아 Southeast Asia 얻다 to gain 중동 the Middle East 널리 widely 열풍 hot wind or fever 감독 producer, director 영화제 film festival 감독상 director award 수출액 amount of export 수준 level 그러다가 while so

통신이나 인터넷**을 통해서**^{GU5.10} 온라인에서 주로 하는 e스포츠가 성장하게 되었다.

이처럼 1990년대부터 크게 성장해 온 한류는 드라마, 음악, 영화, 게임 등 여러 분야에서 찾아볼 수 있다. 지역도 아시아에서 시작해서 미국과 세계 다른 여러 나라에도 알려져 있다. 예전에는 한류를 일시적인 현상으로 생각하는 사람들도 많았지만 지금은 한류가 세계 대중문화의 중요한 부분을 차지**할 정도로**^{GU5.11} 발전했다. 이제는 많은 사람들이 앞으로 한류가 또 어떻게 발전해 나**갈지 기대하고 있다**.^{GU5.12}

일시적 temporary, momentary 기대하다 to anticipate

이해 문제

가... 본문을 읽고 다음 내용이 본문의 내용과 같으면 ○, 틀리면 X에 표시하세요.

1. 한류는 K-pop으로 처음 시작됐다.   ○   X

2. 한국 역사 드라마는 인기를 끌기 어렵다.   ○   X

3. 한국 영화들은 주로 아시아 지역에서 인기를 모으고 있다.   ○   X

4. 2000년부터는 한류의 인기가 떨어지기 시작했다.   ○   X

5. 요즘 한류를 일시적인 현상으로 생각하는 사람들이 늘고 있다.   ○   X

나... 본문을 읽고 다음 질문에 답하세요.

1. 한류란 무엇입니까? 한류의 정의를 써 보세요.

2. 한류는 어떤 분야에서 제일 먼저 시작되었습니까?

3. 한류는 어느 지역에서 처음 시작되었습니까?

4. '대장금'의 성공은 어떤 효과를 가져왔습니까?

5. 음악과 드라마 외에 한류에는 어떤 것이 있나요?

문법과 용법

GU5.8

~다고/라고 보다
                'regard as; consider/think/feel that'

가수들의 너무 심한 경쟁은 문제**라고 봐**.

(I) think too much competition among the singers is a problem.

한류는 1990년대 중반 드라마로 아시아에서 시작되었**다고 본다**.

Hallyu is regarded as having started with soap operas in the mid-1990s in Asia.

나는 그 아이디어가 아주 좋**다고 보는**데요.

I think that is a good idea.

▶ The verb 보다 'see, look at' has extended meanings such as 'think', 'regard (as)', 'consider', and 'feel'. Such extended meanings show up when it occurs after a quotative construction ending in ~다고/라고, where ~다/라 is a plain statement ending and 고 'that' is a quotative particle. The ending ~라 occurs only after the present form of the copula (이), while ~다 occurs after all other forms of predicate, as illustrated in the above example sentences.

GU5.9

~ 겸 'and also, as well as; with the dual purpose of'

이 분은 가수 **겸** 프로듀서예요.

This person is a singer and also a producer.

쇼핑도 하고 박물관도 갈 **겸** 한국에 갔어요.

I went to Korea to do shopping and to go to museums, too.

구경도 할 **겸** 친구도 만날 **겸** 미국에 갔어요.

I went to the U.S. to sightsee and to see my friends, too.

▶ The Sino-Korean bound noun 겸 'combination, addition, concurrence' is used to combine two nouns to express 'and also, as well as'. ~겸 is also used for talking about two actions that take place simultaneously. In this case, the modifier ending is only the prospective ~을/를.

GU5.10

~을/를 통해(서) 'through'

나는 한국에서 경험**을 통해** 많은 것들을 배울 수 있었다.

I was able to learn a lot through my experiences in Korea.

요즘 사람들은 주로 인터넷**을 통해서** 정보를 얻는다.

These days people usually get their information through the Internet.

▶ This pattern expresses ways and means. It combines the object particle 을/를, the verb 통하다 'go through, lead to', and the connective ending ~여 'by, so, and then'. 통해 is a contraction of 통하여.

~(으)ㄹ 정도로 'to the degree/extent to/of ~'

어제는 혼자 일어나지 못**할 정도로** 술을 마셨어.

Yesterday I drank to the extent that I could not stand up on my own.

걷기 힘**들 정도로** 바람이 많이 불어요.

The wind is blowing so much it is difficult to walk.

▶ The Sino-Korean noun 정도 literally means "degree, extent", and this pattern is used when you want to describe a state or action by expressing the degree. This structure is often interchangeable with ~(으)ㄹ 만큼.

~(으)ㄹ지(를) 기대하다
'look forward to, anticipate that ...'

생일에 어떤 선물을 받**을지 기대하**고 있어요.

I am looking forward to what kind of gifts I will get on my birthday.

한국어 대회에서 누가 상을 **탈지** 모두 **기대하고** 있어요.

Everyone is waiting to find out who will win the Korean language contest.

▶ The pattern ~(으)ㄹ지 is an indirect question ending of a question-word or yes-no question clause. Question words include 어떻게, 어떤, 누가, 언제, 무엇, and 어디. The indirect question clause functions as the object of the transitive verb in the main clause. The main transitive verbs include 알다, 모르다, 기대하다, and 예상하다. 기대하다 means 'to look forward to, expect, anticipate something'. Looking forward to something with an anticipation involves non-realized or prospective situations. Thus, the probable/possible ~(으)ㄹ지 is used, rather than the present ~(으)ㄴ지 or the past ~었/았는지.

활동

가... 다음 빈 칸에 가장 어울리는 단어를 고르세요.

1. 일반적으로 한류는 1990년대 아시아에서 시작되었다고 _____.

   ㄱ. 알렸다   ㄴ. 보인다   ㄷ. 알았다   ㄹ. 본다

2. 한류 때문에 한국 연예인이 일본에서 큰 인기를 _____.

   ㄱ. 있다   ㄴ. 얻었다   ㄷ. 높았다   ㄹ. 대단하다

3. 최근 비빔밥과 김치 같은 한식이 세계에 널리 _____.

   ㄱ. 알았다   ㄴ. 알게 됐다   ㄷ. 알려졌다   ㄹ. 얻었다

4. 한류는 이제 아시아_____ 세계적으로 인기를 끌고 있다.

   ㄱ. 널리   ㄴ. 도   ㄷ. 는 물론이고   ㄹ. 에서밖에

5. 한류는 음식은 물론이고 드라마, 음악, 영화, 게임 등 여러 _____에서 찾아볼 수 있다.

   ㄱ. 분야   ㄴ. 지역   ㄷ. 전체   ㄹ. 나라

나... 다음 대화를 완성해 보세요.

1. ㄱ: K-pop이 왜 인기라고 생각하세요?

   ㄴ: 저는 _____다고/라고 봐요.

2. ㄱ: 실례지만 어떤 일을 하세요?

   ㄴ: 저는 _____ 겸 _____입니다.

3. ㄱ: 한국에서 일을 하고 싶은데 취업 정보를 어디에서 얻을 수 있나요?

   ㄴ: _____을/를 통해서 알아볼 수 있어요.

4. ㄱ: 이 영화 어땠어요?

   ㄴ: _____ 정도로 감동적이었어요.

5. ㄱ: 한국과 브라질의 축구 경기에서 한국 팀의 성적을 어떻게 예상하십니까?

   ㄴ: 네, 한국 팀이 _____지 기대하고 있습니다.

라... 한국 영화나 드라마에서 가장 자주 나오는 소재 (subject matter; material) 는
무엇이 있습니까? 한 가지씩 설명해 보세요.

   1. _____

   2. _____

   3. _____

   4. _____

   5. _____

마… 다음 질문에 대해 한 문단 정도로 써 본 뒤 토론해 보세요.

1. 요즘 인기 있는 한국의 영화, 드라마, 노래, 연예인에 대해 조사를 한 뒤 하나를 선택해서 자세히 써 보세요.

2. 한류가 성공한 이유는 무엇이라고 생각합니까?

3. 한류는 어떻게 성장해 왔습니까? 한 문단 정도 써 보세요.

4. 한류가 앞으로 어떻게 발전해 나갈지 여러분의 기대나 생각을 써 보세요.

추가 읽기

한류의 힘과 영향

한류는 1990년대에 중국, 일본, 동남아 등지에서 시작해 미주, 유럽, 호주, 아프리카, 중동 등 세계로 퍼져 나가고 있다. 특히 한국 드라마가 한류에서 큰 비중을 차지하고 있는데 많은 사람들이 중독성이 있다고 이야기할 정도로 인기가 많다. 한국 드라마가 많은 사랑을 받는 이유 중 하나는 상상을 초월하는 기발한 소재 때문인데 다음 다섯 가지는 한국 드라마에서 자주 나오는 소재들이라고 한다.

1. 음식 이야기: 드라마마다 맛있게 보이는 다양한 한국 음식들이 등장하여 드라마 팬들의 관심을 끌고 있다.
2. 교통사고: 교통사고를 당해 기억을 잃어버리는 등의 이야기가 자주 이용된다.
3. 인기가 많은 주제곡: 드라마 주제곡들이 K-pop 차트에서 높은 순위를 차지할 때가 많고 아이돌 가수가 직접 드라마에 나오기도 한다.
4. 유행 타는 소재: 한국 드라마들의 이야기들은 유행을 타는데, 어떤 시기에는 시간 여행, 또 한동안은 뱀파이어, 이후에는

등지 and other places 미주 the Americas 퍼져 나가다 to spread out 중독성 addiction
상상을 초월하다 to go beyond imagination 기발하다 to be brilliant, novel 소재 subject
matter; material 교통사고 traffic accident 당하다 to fall victim to something 기억 memory
주제곡 theme song 유행을 타다 to go along the trend

여장 남자(남장 여자) 같은 소재들이 유행하며 반복되기도 한다.

5. 로맨틱한 사랑 이야기: 사랑 고백이 많은 한국 드라마의 중요한 주
제인데 보통 사랑이 아주 조금씩 진행되다 결국 "나 너 많이 좋아
해"라고 말하는 식의 이야기가 자주 나온다.

한국방송광고진흥공사에 따르면 드라마의 영향으로 한국 상품들이 많이
팔리고, 드라마 촬영지를 방문하는 외국인들이 많아지고, 한국어를 공부하
는 사람들도 늘어났다고 한다. 배우들이 방송에 입고 나오는 옷은 물론이
고 가방, 액세서리도 한국을 여행하는 외국인 관광객들에게 큰 인기를 끌
고 있다.

반복 repetition 고백 confession 진행되다 to progress 한국방송광고진흥공사 Korea
Broadcast Advertising Corporation 늘어나다 to increase

문화

서울의 한류 명소

한류의 영향으로 한국을 여행하는 외국인 관광객 수도 많이 늘었다. 한류 팬들이 많이 찾는 서울의 명소로는 다음과 같은 곳들이 있다.

N서울타워

남산 정상에 있는 N서울타워는 높이 236.7m, 해발 497.7m의 탑이다. 이곳 7층의 식당은 360° 회전하며 이곳에서 서울 시내를 한눈에 볼 수 있다. 특히 야경이 아름다워 많은 드라마가 이곳에서 촬영되었고 데이트를 즐기려는 연인들이 많이 찾는 곳이다.

정상 summit 탑 tower 해발 above sea level 회전 turn or revolve 야경 night view

경복궁

경복궁은 조선 시대 궁궐인데 많은 사극들이 이곳에서 촬영되었다. 경복궁 근처에는 한복을 빌려주는 곳도 있어서 많은 외국인들이 한복을 입고 경복궁을 구경하는 모습을 볼 수 있다.

남산골 한옥마을

한국의 전통 집들이 모여 있는 남산골 한옥마을은 텔레비전 프로그램에 자주 등장해 외국 관광객들에게 인기 있는 장소이다.

궁궐 palace 사극 historical drama 빌려주다 to lend 구경 sightseeing 모습 looks or appearance 전통 tradition 등장하다 to make an appearance

여의도 한강 공원 및 한강 유람선

많은 드라마의 연인들이 데이트를 즐기는 여의도 한강 공원에는 벚꽃 축제, 세계 불꽃 축제 등 연중 다양한 행사가 열린다. 여의도에서 출발하는 한강 유람선도 로맨틱한 데이트 장소로 유명하다.

한류 스타 거리

한류 스타 거리(K-Star Road)는 한류 스타들의 이미지를 더한 대형 인형을 전시해 놓은 거리이다. SM, YG, JYP 등 유명한 엔터테인먼트 회사들이 근처에 있어 운이 좋으면 실제로 스타를 볼 수도 있다.

http://korean.visitseoul.net/hallyu-recommend (서울 특별시 웹사이트 참조)

벚꽃 cherry blossoms 불꽃(놀이) fireworks 연중 year-round 상징화하다 to symbolize
인형 조형물 iconic doll sculptures 전시하다 to display or exhibit 운이 좋다 to be lucky

▌▌ 번역문 ▌▌

CONVERSATION: *Hallyu* and Korean Courses

In a classroom before the class starts

Chiyun: Have you been watching Korean dramas lately?

Sandy: No, when you start watching a drama you can't stop, so I'm planning on watching them during the break.

Minjun: I never thought Sandy would watch Korean dramas ...

Sandy: That's what I thought, too ... Of all the people, I never thought I'd become a Korean idol fan, let alone (watch) Korean dramas.

Mark: That's why instead of dramas, I watch a lot of movies. I like historical movies, and while watching the movies "Taegukgi" and "Ode to My Father" (*lit.* International Market) I ended up learning more about the Korean War.

Chiyun: Wow! Isn't history hard?

Mark: Oh, no, you should watch it, too. (When you do,) you cannot help but become interested in Korean history. I am going to take a Korean history class next semester.

Minjun: I heard that in the modern Korean culture course, there's stuff about idol groups.

Sandy: Really? I'm a fan of Korean idol groups. They are really good dancers! I went to a lot of their concerts in the U.S.

Minjun: (In that class), I think you learn about the training the idol groups undergo before their debut and the reasons for *Hallyu* catching on in other countries.

Mark: Now that I think about it, the scope of *Hallyu* is quite broad. There're movies, dramas, and K-pop, of course, and food and fashion are also included, you know. Also, online games and video games are really famous throughout the world.

Chiyun: That's true. *Hallyu's* economic effect is probably big too. Tourists often visit the places where dramas or movies were filmed, and it's said that products that celebrities advertise sell well. Products that celebrities use sell well too.

Sandy: Right. N Seoul Tower became more famous because they filmed dramas there. I went there last year, and there were a lot of foreign tourists.

Chiyun: How about if we take the Korean culture class together next semester?

Minjun: Of course!

Sandy: Me, too! If you guys are taking it, I'll have to take it, too!

Mark: I'm going to take a history course, but I'll take the Korean culture class if there isn't a time conflict with my other classes.

READING: The Growth of Korean Wave and Its History

The term "Hallyu" refers to the phenomenon of Korean culture becoming popular abroad. Generally, *Hallyu* is seen as having started with Korean dramas in Asia during the mid-1990s. As such, the *Hallyu* which started with dramas, expanded when in the late 1990s dance groups like Clon and H.O.T. became popular in China. Then, groups like TVXQ were created targeting all of Asia. Since then, singers famous for their dancing became prominent. After that, Rain became very popular in 2002, and BoA became very popular in Japan in 2003. Subsequently, in 2004 singer and actress Jang Na-ra became popular in China. In 2007, the hip hop group Big Bang succeeded in Japan. Additionally starting in 2009, girl groups like the Wonder Girls and Girls' Generation started to gain popularity overseas. Fan clubs and Korean entertainment companies such as SM, YG, and MYP played a major role in the success of idol stars.

Hallyu went beyond Asia, by also becoming popular in the U.S. In 2012, Psy's "Gangnam Style" made it to the second place on the U.S. Billboard Top 100 chart and had almost 3 billion hits on YouTube. Furthermore, in 2017 the boy band Bangtan Sonyeondan (Bulletproof Boy Scouts, BTS) continued the Korean Wave with their hit song that rose to America's Billboard Top 100 chart.

Dramas, too have remained popular, and in 2000 "Autumn in My Heart" was popular in Southeast Asia. In 2004, "Winter Sonata" was broadcasted on NHK TV in Japan, gaining a great deal of popularity. The same year, the Korean food themed historical drama "Jewel in the Palace" became popular not just in Asia, but in the U.S., the Middle East, and Africa as well. It was broadcasted in about 90 countries. Through the influence of "Jewel in the Palace," Korean foods like *pibimbap* and kimchi became well known throughout the world. In fusion cooking in other countries, the use of Korea's *koch'ujang* red pepper paste and kimchi can often be seen.

Movies are also an important aspect when it comes to *Hallyu*. Movies like "My Sassy Girl", "Taegeukgi", and "Shiri" contributed to the *Hallyu* craze. Additionally, "Sopyonje " by director Im Kwon-taek has won awards at famous international film festivals like the Cannes Film Festival, Venice Film Festival, and the Berlin Film Festival. Korean games have also become popular worldwide. The volume of exports in Korean games is 11 times larger than that of K-pop. Gaming in Korea started with video games in the mid-1970s, and at that time Korean games were at a stage where they were following the games of other countries. Then, from the late 1980s on, Korean made games such as The Legend of Sword came out, and the types of games also gradually increased. Subsequently, Starcraft champion Lim Yo-hwan and many other professional gamers appeared, and e-Sports — mainly played online through computer communications or the Internet — grew.

As such, *Hallyu* can be found in a variety of areas including dramas, music, movies, games, etc. Region-wise, too, *Hallyu* has also reached the United States and other countries around the world, after having started in Asia. In the past, many people thought that *Hallyu* was a temporary phenomenon, but now *Hallyu* has developed to the point that it has taken its place as an important part of the global pop culture. Now, many people look forward to how *Hallyu* will develop in the future.

FURTHER READING: The Power and Influence of *Hallyu*

Hallyu started in China, Japan and Southeast Asia in the 1990s, and is now spreading around the world to places like the Americas, Europe, Australia, Africa, and the Middle East, etc. Korean dramas in particular have had a major influence on *Hallyu*, to the extent that people say that Korean dramas are addictive. One of the reasons for the popularity is the subject matter goes beyond one's imagination. The following five subject matters are said to be commonly found in Korean dramas:

1. Food Stories: Various delicious-looking Korean foods appear in each drama and attract the interest of drama fans.
2. Traffic Accidents: Stories such as people having traffic accidents and then suffering memory loss are frequently featured.
3. Popular Theme Music: There are many instances in which theme songs from dramas move high up on the K-pop charts and/or an idol singer appears directly in the drama.
4. Trendy Subject Matter: The stories of Korean dramas follow the current fads. For a time, themes such as time travel become popular, then vampires were popular for a while, then later men dressing as women (women dressing as men). Then the themes are repeated when they become popular again.
5. Romantic Love Stories: Confession of one's love is an important theme in many Korean dramas. In many stories, love usually progresses little by little until the end, when one character comes out with, "I like you a lot."

According to the Korea Broadcast Advertising Corporation (KOBACO), the influence of dramas has brought about high volume of sales of Korean products, a rise in foreign tourists visiting the locations where dramas were filmed, and an increase in the number of people studying Korean. Also, along with the clothing worn in shows, the bags and accessories used by actors and actresses are popular with foreign tourists traveling in Korea

CULTURE: Seoul's *Hallyu* Attractions

The number of foreign tourists who traveled to Korea because of the influence of *Hallyu* has increased greatly. The following are some of the most popular places in Seoul where *Hallyu* fans are visiting.

1. Namsan Seoul Tower (NSeoul Tower)
Located on top of Namsan Mountain, Namsan Seoul Tower is 236.7m high and 497.7m above sea level. The restaurant on the 7th floor revolves 360°, and you can see Seoul's downtown at a glance. Since the night view is especially beautiful,

many dramas have been shot here, and many couples go here on dates.

2. Gyeongbokgung

Gyeongbokgung is a palace of the Chŏsun Dynasty, and many historical dramas have been filmed here. There are places to borrow *hanbok*, or Korean costumes near Gyeongbokgung, so many foreign tourists can be seen touring the Palace wearing a *hanbok*.

3. Namsan'gol Hanok Village

Namsan'gol Hanok Village, where many Korean traditional houses are located together is a popular sightseeing spot for foreign tourists because of its appearance on many television programs.

4. Yeouido Han'gang Park and Han'gang Ferry Cruise

Yeouido Han'gang Park is where couples in many dramas enjoy going on dates. At the park, various events such as the Yeouido Spring Blossom Festival and the Seoul International Fireworks Festival are held throughout the year. The Han'gang Ferry Cruise from Yeouido is also a famous place to enjoy a romantic date.

5. K-Star Road

K-Star Road is a street displaying large bear doll figures characterizing K-pop stars. Famous entertainment companies such as SM, YG and JYP are nearby, so if you get lucky, you can actually see the stars.

■■ 단어 ■■

감독	producer, director	벚꽃	cherry blossoms
감독상	director award	분야	area, field
겹치다	to overlap, double	불꽃(놀이)	fireworks
고백	confession	빌려주다	to lend
공연	performance	사극	historical drama
교통사고	traffic accident	상대방	the other (party)
구경	sightseeing	상상을 초월하다	to go beyond imagination
궁궐	palace	상징화하다	to symbolize
그러다가	while so	상품	products
그만두다	to stop, quit	성공하다	to be successful
기대하다	to anticipate	성장	growth
기발하다	to be brilliant, novel	소재	subject matter; material
기억	memory	수준	level
너희들	you (guys)	수출액	amount of export
널리	widely	시장	market
1990년대	1990s	아이돌	teen idol
늘어나다	to increase	야경	night view
당연하지!	Of course!	얻다	to gain
당하다	to fall victim to something	역할을 하다	to play a role
대중	public; mass	연예인	entertainer
더 나아가	furthermore	연중	year-round
동남아시아	Southeast Asia	열풍	hot wind or fever
두각을 나타내다	to distinguish oneself	영향	effect, influence
등장하다	to make an appearance	영화제	film festival
등지	and other places	운이 좋다	to be lucky
모습	looks or appearance	유행을 타다	to go along the trend
미주	the Americas	이유	reason
반복	repetition	인형 조형물	iconic doll sculptures
범위	scope, range	일시적	temporary, momentary

전시하다	to display or exhibit	토론	discussion, debate
전통	tradition	퍼져 나가다	to spread out
전혀	(not) at all	포함하다	to include
전체	the whole	한국전쟁	Korean War
정상	summit	한국방송광고	Korea Broadcast
조회 수	number of views or searches	진흥공사	Advertising Corporation
주제곡	theme song	해발	above sea level
중독성	addiction	해외	overseas
중동	the Middle East	현상	phenomenon
중반	the middle phase	회전	turn or revolve
진행되다	to progress	효과	effect
촬영지	filming site	훈련	training, drill
촬영하다	to film		
탑	tower		
태극기 휘날리며	the movie "Taegukgi, Brotherhood of War" (*lit.* Fluttering the Korean Flag)		

6과

호칭어와 대인 관계

Lesson 6 Address Terms and Interpersonal Relations

학습 목표

내용
- 한국 사람들이 대인 관계에서 서로를 부르는 호칭어의 종류를 알아본다.
- 다양한 호칭어의 적절한 사용법을 배운다.

문화
- 호칭어 사용을 통하여 한국인의 가치관이 다른 문화와 어떻게 다른지 알아본다.
- 가족 관계와 직장의 구조를 배운다.

호칭어 address terms 대인 관계 interpersonal relations 부르다 to call 적절하다 to be appropriate 사용법 usage 가치관 values 관계 relationship 구조 structure

■ 생각해 봅시다

가 ▸▸ 다음에 대해 이야기해 봅시다.

　　1. 호칭어와 지칭어는 어떻게 다릅니까? 영어와 한국어에서 예를 들어
　　　말해 보세요.

　　2. 한국 사람들과 말할 때 호칭어나 지칭어 사용 때문에 실수한 적이
　　　있으면 말해 보세요.

나 ▸▸ 다음 말에서 어느 단어가 호칭어이고 어느 단어가 지칭어입니까?

　　1. 금복아, 할머니 모시고 가라.

　　2. 아빠, 엄마를 좀 이해해 주세요.

　　3. 윤 교수님, 오랜만이에요.

　　4. 저기, 김 사장님 오세요.

지칭어 reference terms 모시다 to accompany; to serve under 사장 company president

다 ▸ 다음 상황에서 상대방을 어떻게 부르는 것이 좋은지 여러분 문화와
　　비교해서 대답하세요.

　　1. 식당에서 손님이 종업원을 부를 때:

　　2. 은행에서 직원이 손님을 부를 때:

　　3. 병원에서 환자가 의사를 부를 때:

　　4. 병원에서 환자가 간호사를 부를 때:

　　5. 길을 묻기 위해서 사람을 부를 때:

　　6. 학교에서 선배나 후배를 부를 때:

　　7. 남편과 아내가 서로를 부를 때:

　　8. 남자 친구와 여자 친구가 서로를 부를 때:

상황 situation 직원 clerk, employee 환자 patient 간호사 nurse 남편 husband 아내 wife

김 부장과 이 대리

컴퓨터 회사 김지호 부장(남)과 이준기 대리(남)가
일요일에 백화점에서 마주쳤다

이 대리: (여자 옷을 보고 있는 김 부장에게) 부장**님**,^{GU6.1} 안녕하세요?

김 부장: **아니**,^{GU6.2} 이 대리, 백화점에는 어떻게?

이 대리: 저희 집 애가 친구들하고 도봉산에 간**다기에**^{GU6.3} 등산화 한
켤레^{GU6.4} 사 줄까 하고요.

얘, 민호야, 인사 드려라. 아빠 회사 부장님이시다.

민호: 안녕하세요.

김 부장: 응, 민호 안녕. 민호 아주 잘생겼구나.
아빠 붕어빵이네. 몇 학년이지?

민호: 초등학교 3학년이에요.

이 대리: 그런데 부장님은 어떻게 나오셨습니까?

김 부장: 난 시카고에 있는 딸애한테 겨울 옷 두어 벌 사 보낼까 하
고. 집사람이 곧 딸 보러 시카고에 간다기에.

아, 여기 집사람 오네요.

여보, 우리 회사 이준기 대리예요. 아주 유능한 분인데 아들

마주치다 to come across 부장 division chief 남 male 대리 deputy section chief 등산화
hiking shoes 켤레 a pair (of hand and foot wear) 인사 드리다 to greet a senior
딸애 = 딸아이 daughter 두어 a couple of 집사람 my wife 유능하다 to be competent

등산화 사러 나왔대요.

이 대리: 사모님, 처음 뵙겠습니다. 이준기입니다. 부장님을 모시고 있습니다.

김 부장 부인: 반가워요, 이 대리님.

아드님이 아주 귀여워요. 아빠를 많이 닮았네요.

이 대리: 다들 그러더라고요.

김 부장: 그럼, 바쁠 텐데^{GU6.5} 어서 등산화 보러 가 보지 그래요.^{GU6.6} 이 대리, 반가웠어요.

이 대리: 네, 그러겠습니다.

그럼, 먼저 실례하겠습니다.

민호야, 가자.

민호: 네, 아빠.

(김 부장 부부에게) 안녕히 가세요.

김 부장 부부: 그래, 민호야 잘 가.

(잠시 후)

이 대리: 아, 저기 차수빈 씨도 오네! 차수빈 씨!

차수빈: 어머, 안녕하세요, 이 대리님!

이 대리: 쇼핑하러 나오셨나 봐요?

차수빈: 네, 친구들이랑 뭐 좀^{GU6.7} 사러 나왔어요.

이 대리: 그럼, 쇼핑 잘 하시고 내일 회사에서 봐요.

차수빈: 네, 내일 뵙겠습니다.

사모님 one's teacher's or senior's wife 아드님 one's senior's son 어서 quickly, please
그러겠다 =그렇게 하겠다 실례하다 to be excused 잠시 후 after a while 어머 (feminine
exclamation) Oh, my! 뭐(=뭣) something 좀 just

이해 문제

가... 다음 내용이 대화의 내용과 같으면 ○, 다르면 X에 표시하세요.

1. 김 부장과 이 대리는 컴퓨터 회사에서 일한다.   ○   X

2. 김 부장은 아들의 등산화를 사러 왔다.   ○   X

3. 김 부장의 가족들은 모두 시카고에 산다.   ○   X

4. 민호는 아빠를 붕어빵처럼 닮았다.   ○   X

5. 차수빈 씨는 혼자서 쇼핑하러 나왔다.   ○   X

나... 다음 질문에 대답해 보세요.

1. 이 대리는 무엇을 사려고 누구하고 백화점에 나왔습니까?

2. 김 부장은 누구하고 왜 백화점에 왔습니까?

3. 이 대리는 김 부장의 부인에게 왜 부장님을 "모시고 있다"라는 표현을 썼을까요?

4. 이 대리와 차수빈 씨는 서로 어떻게 아는 사이라고 생각하세요?

5. 대화에 나오는 호칭어와 지칭어들을 찾아 적고 어떤 상황에서 쓰였는지
　　말해 봅시다.

　　　　ㄱ: _____

　　　　ㄴ: _____

　　　　ㄷ: _____

　　　　ㄹ: _____

　　　　ㅁ: _____

　　　　ㅂ: _____

　　　　ㅅ: _____

문법과 용법

~님 'Mr./Mrs./Ms., honorable'

▶ This is the highest and most frequently used honorific title suffix. Unlike English title prefixes (Mr., Ms., etc.), it is usually attached to a job title or a kinship term, as in 사장님 'Mr./Ms. President', 기사님 'Mr./Ms. Driver', 김 박사님 'Dr. Kim', and 아버님 '(honorable) father'. It is essential to use "–님" to address or refer to a non-kin senior person or distant equal. Not using it implies that the speaker considers the addressee or referent as his/her subordinate or close equal. Among family members, using –님 sounds very formal. Thus, one often uses 아빠, 아버지 to one's own father, but 아버님 to one's in-laws. 누님, 형님 sound more formal than 누나, 형.

아니 'dear me, why, what, good heavens, well, oh'

아니, 이 대리, 백화점에는 어떻게?
Oh! Mr. Lee, what brings you to the department store?

아니, 이 사람 누구야?!
Dear me, who's this?

▶ The negative adverb 아니 'not' usually modifies a predicate, but it is also used as a sentence adverb or discourse particle to indicate the unexpectedness of the situation and the speaker's surprise. As a sentence adverb, it is placed in the beginning of the sentence.

~다기에 'because, for, since, as someone said that'

월세가 오른**다기에**(or 오른다길래) 다음 학기부터는 기숙사에 살려고 해요.
I am planning to live in the dorms starting next semester because I heard rent is going to go up.

비가 온**다기에** (or 온다길래) 밖에 나가지 않았어요.
I didn't go out since I heard it was going to rain.

친구가 돈이 없**다기에**(or 없다길래) 빌려주었어.
I lent money to a friend as he said he does not have money.

▶ This is a case of 고 하 'say that' deletion from –다고 하기에, a frequent phenomenon in spoken Korean. –다 is a declarative ending of a quoted clause (–다 changes to –라 if the clause has the present form of the copula, as in 학생이라기에 'as he/she/someone said he/she is a student'). –기에 consists of the nominalizer suffix –기, and the particle 에 'at, on, in, for'. Thus, the literal meaning of ~다기에 is 'for (someone's) saying that'. In spoken Korean, –기에 can be replaced by –길래, as in ~다길래.

> GU6.4

Numeral classifiers (or counters)

▶ In counting objects, Koreans use not only numbers, but also bound nouns called classifiers or counters after the numbers. Depending on the properties of the objects counted, different classifiers are used, as illustrated below.

Unit being counted	Classifier	Example
things in general	개 'item'	사과/돌/책상 한 개
clothes	벌	옷/양복/바지/등산복 세 벌
shoes, socks, gloves	켤레 'pair'	신/구두/등산화/양말 한 켤레
books	권	책/사전/교과서 다섯 권
paper, ticket	장 'sheet'	종이/차표 두 장
vehicles, machines	대	비행기/컴퓨터/차 한 대
animals, insects	마리	개/소/파리 여러 마리
people	사람, 명, 분(honorific)	학생/남자 세 사람/명 선생님/어른/노인 세 분
houses	채	집/건물/아파트 열 채
buildings	동	아파트 다섯 동
liquid in cups/glasses	잔 'cup/glass'	술/커피 한 잔
liquid in bottles	병 'bottle'	맥주/소주 한 병
boats and ships	척	배/보트 세 척
long slender objects	자루	연필/비(broom) 두 자루
grapes, bananas, flowers	송이 'bunch, cluster'	장미 한 송이, 포도 다섯 송이

GU6.5

~(으)ㄹ 텐데
'I guess; I think; I'm sure that ..., (so, but)'

바쁘실 **텐데** 와 주셔서 감사합니다.

Thank you for coming even though I'm sure you must be busy.

비가 **올 텐데** 우산을 가지고 가세요.

I think it's going to rain, so you should take an umbrella with you.

▶ This pattern expresses the speaker's guess or conjecture of a state or event. The content of the clause before the pattern is what the speaker guesses. This pattern is a combination of –(으)ㄹ 터 'the situation that (some event/state) may', the copula 이, and the connective ending –ㄴ데 'in the circumstance that'. Thus, the literal meaning is 'in the circumstance that the situation is that (some state or event) may'.

GU6.6

~지 그래(요) 'how about ...?'

빨리 자고 내일 아침 일찍 일어나**지 그래**.

How about going to bed now and then getting up early tomorrow morning?

지금 떠나시**지 그러세요**.

How about departing now?

▶ This pattern occurs only after a verb and indicates the speaker's polite suggestion toward the listener. It appears to be a contraction of ~지 않고 그래(요) 'why do you do so without doing...' with the deletion of 않고 'without doing'. To a senior person, ~지 그러세요 is used.

~ 좀 'just; a little; please'

친구들이랑 뭐 **좀** 사러 왔어요.

I came with friends to buy a few things.

문 **좀** 닫아 주세요.

Would you please shut the door?

언제 시간 **좀** 내 주세요.

Could you please make time for me sometime?

▶ The "discourse" particle 좀 has derived via contraction from the noun/adverb 조금 'a small amount, slightly, somewhat'. In addition to the noun/adverb meanings, it functions to indicate the speaker's humble or polite attitude by softening the assertion or utterance tone. It can be translated as 'just, a little' (in statement and question) and 'please, would you, kindly' (in proposal and request). As a discourse particle, it can appear after any word in a sentence.

활동

가... 대화에서 나온 호칭어를 여러분 언어의 호칭어로 바꾸어 보세요.

나... 다음 대화에서 잘못된 표현을 찾아 고쳐 보세요.

김 부장: 이 대리, 내가 좀 할 말이 있는데.

이 대리: 네, 김 부장님, 언제 뵐 수 있겠습니까?

김 부장: 좀 뒤에 윤 대리님하고 차수빈을 데리고 내 사무실로 오세요.

이 대리: 그러겠습니다, 김 부장님.

_____ → _____

_____ → _____

다... 다음 단어들을 셀 때 필요한 분류사(counter)에 줄을 그어 연결해 보세요.

장갑 •	• 권
주스 •	• 마리
잡지 •	• 대
새 •	• 켤레
점원 •	• 분
청바지 •	• 자루
피아노 •	• 잔
목사님 •	• 벌
군함 •	• 척
포도주 •	• 병
연필 •	• 명

라... 다음 수+분류사 앞에 쓸 수 있는 단어를 써 보세요.

곰 세 마리

1. _____ 한 병   2. _____ 두 대

3. _____ 다섯 채   4. _____ 열 명

5. _____ 스무 개   6. _____ 다섯 송이

7. _____ 네 분

마... 주어진 표현을 사용하여 대화를 완성해 보세요.

1. ~다기에

ㄱ: 한국어 수업 왜 들어요?

ㄴ: _____ .

2. ~(으)ㄹ 텐데

ㄱ: 스티브 생일 파티를 어디서 하는 게 좋을까요?

ㄴ: _____ .

3. ~지 그래요

ㄱ: 감기 걸려서 지금 고생이에요. 일주일이나 됐는데…

ㄴ: _____ .

바... 다음과 같은 대화를 만들어 옆 사람과 말해 보세요.

1. 오랫동안 못 만난 선배를 학교에서 만났습니다.

   ㄱ. 인사를 하세요.

   ㄴ. 그동안 어떻게 지냈는지 이야기해 보세요.

   ㄷ. 주말 계획을 물어 보세요.

   ㄹ. 만날 약속을 하세요.

2. 같은 수업을 듣는 친구를 월요일에 길에서 만났습니다.

   ㄱ. 인사를 하세요.

   ㄴ. 주말에 무엇을 했는지 서로 이야기해 보세요.

   ㄷ. 같이 듣는 수업의 공부/숙제에 대해서 이야기해 보세요.

   ㄹ. 같이 만나서 공부할 약속을 해 보세요.

3. 선생님께 전화를 합니다. 전화로 추천서를 부탁하려고 합니다.

   ㄱ. 선생님께 인사를 하세요.

   ㄴ. 선생님께 어떻게 지내시는지 안부를 여쭤 보세요.

   ㄷ. 무슨 추천서가 필요한지 이야기하고 부탁을 하세요.

   ㄹ. 언제 선생님을 찾아뵐 것인지 약속을 하세요.

읽기

한국인의 호칭 문화

일상 생활에서 대화할 때 언어 예절이 필요하다. 언어 예절 중^{GU6.8} 하나는 상대방을 부르는 방법이다. 상대방을 부르는 말을 호칭어라고 하는데, 한국어는 영어에 비해서 상당히 복잡하고 다양한 호칭어가 있다. 호칭어 사용은 존대법과 함께 대인 관계에서 가장 민감한 언어 예절이다. 호칭어는 말하는 사람과 듣는 사람의 관계를 나타낸다. 적절한 호칭어 사용은 대화를 순조롭게 하고 대화하는 사람들의 관계를 부드럽게 해 준다.

호칭어는 크게 친족어와 비친족어로 나눌 수 있다. 친족어에는 "아버지, 어머니, 형, 언니" 같은 호칭이 있다. 예를 들어, 며느리를 부를 때 "새아가" "어멈아"라고 하고, 남편을 부를 때 "오빠" "아빠" "여보"나 "[자녀 이름] 아빠"라고 한다.

한국 사회의 특징 중 하나는 친족이 아닌 사람들에게도 친족어를 사용하는 것이다. 이것은 친밀함을 표현하기 위한 것인데, 친구의 부모님을 "아버님, 어머님"이라 부르고, 학교 선배를 "형" 또는 "언니"라고 부를 수 있다. 다른 한편으로는 상업 전략으로 사용하기도 한다. 백화점이나 음식점 점원은 고객을 "아버님, 어머님, 언니"라고 불러서 손님의 마음을 끈다. 손님은 여자 점원을 보통 "언니"나 "이

언어 예절 language etiquette 상당히 considerably 존대법 honorifics 민감하다 to be sensitive 순조롭다 to be smooth 친족어 kinship terms 비친족어 non-kin terms 며느리 daughter-in-law 자녀 children, sons and daughters 친밀함 intimacy 상업 전략 sales tactic 점원 clerk (of a store) 고객 customer 마음을 끌다 to attract, allure

모"라고 부르기도 한다.

　　비친족어는 아주 다양하다. **윗사람**이나^{GU6.9} 가깝지 않은 사람에게는 "선생님, 교수님, 사장님" 같은 '직함+님'이 널리 쓰이는데, 그 앞에 이름을 넣어 "김(영수) 선생님" 같이 쓰기도 한다. **아랫사람**이나 ^{GU6.8} 가까운 동료에게는 "김용수 씨, 김 선생, 김 과장"과 같이 이름에 '씨'나 직함을 붙여서 쓴다. 학교나 직장 선배에게는 "선배(님)" 또는 "김 선배(님)"으로 부르는 것이 보통이다. 아이들을 부를 때는 "희정아, 수미야"처럼 이름을 부르는데, 자음으로 끝난 이름에는 "아", 모음으로 끝난 이름에는 "야"를 붙인다. 그 외에도 이름이나 직함을 모르는 사람에게는 상대방의 나이나 상황에 따라 "학생", **"저기요"**, **"여기요"**, ^{GU6.10} "손님", "고객님"이라고 부르기도 한다.

　　한국어**와는 달리**^{GU6.11} 영어에서는 일상 대화에서 남녀노소**를 막론하고**^{GU6.12} 이름을 줄여서 많이 부른다. 성명이 Timothy Smith라면 "Tim"이고 Christine Haig라면 "Chris"로 호칭하는 것이다. 이렇게 이름을 줄여서 사용하면 서로 친밀하고 부드러운 관계를 유지할 수 있기 때문에 많은 사람들은 대화에서 서로가 직함 없이 줄인 이름으로 불러 달라고 한다.

　　영어를 사용하는 사람들은 평등주의와 개인주의 안에서 질서를 유지하**는 반면,**^{GU6.13} 한국 사람들은 어느 정도의 계층주의와 집단주의 안에서 조화를 유지한다. 대인 관계에서 영어 호칭어 사용에 비해, 한국어 호칭어 사용이 복잡해진 배경에는 이런 대조적인 문화가 있다. 이러한 한국인의 인간관계 때문에 한국어의 존대법도 발달했다.

이모 aunt (mom's sister) 직함 job title 자음 consonant 모음 vowel 붙이다 to attach
남녀노소 men and women of all ages 줄이다 to reduce 성명 full name 평등주의
egalitarianism 개인주의 individualism 질서 (social) order 유지하다 to maintain
계층주의 hierarchism 집단주의 collectivism 조화 harmony 대조적 contrastive 인간관계
human relations

이해 문제

가... 다음 내용이 본문의 내용과 같으면 ○, 다르면 X에 표시하세요.

1. 대화할 때 상대방을 부르는 말을 호칭어라 한다.　　　　　○　　　X

2. 한국어에 비해서 영어는 호칭어가 상당히 복잡하다.　　　　○　　　X

3. 친족어는 상업 전략으로만 사용한다.　　　　　　　　　　○　　　X

4. 남편을 "오빠"라고 부를 수 있다.　　　　　　　　　　　○　　　X

5. 윗사람에게는 '직함 + 님'이 널리 쓰인다.　　　　　　　○　　　X

6. 한국어에서는 이름을 줄여서 많이 부른다.　　　　　　　○　　　X

나... 다음 질문에 대답해 보세요.

1. 한국의 대인 관계에서 언어 예절을 가장 잘 표현하는 것은 무엇입니까?

2. 한국 사람들은 왜 친족이 아닌 사람들에게도 친족어를 많이 사용합니까?

3. 한국어의 친족어에는 어떤 것들이 있습니까?

4. 비친족어의 예로는 어떤 것들이 있습니까?

5. 한국어 호칭어가 영어보다 복잡한 이유는 무엇입니까?

문법과 용법

GU6.8

~중(에서) 'among, out of'

한국어를 배우는 이유 **중** 하나는 한국 대중문화를 좋아하기 때문이다.

One of the reasons I'm learning Korean is because I like Korean pop culture.

우리 반 학생 **중에서** 누가 제일 키가 커요?

Who is the tallest among the students in our class?

가: 제니가 수업에 왜 안 왔지?

     Why didn't Jenny come to class?

나: 십중팔구 늦잠 잤을거야.

     I'll bet she overslept.

▶ This pattern is used when one or more is chosen among many others. 중 is a Sino-Korean bound noun meaning 'center, middle, during, among'. It is frequently used as a contraction of 중에서 'from among, out of', as in this pattern. As a bound noun, 중 compounds with many other Sino-Korean nouns, as in 중국 'China', 중학교 'middle school, during, among', 중심 'center', 중간 'middle, halfway' and 십중팔구 '(*lit.* 8 or 9 out of ten) most likely'.

▶ A related pattern ~중(에) 'in the middle of (an event)' is preceded by a clause denoting an event or by a Sino-Korean activity noun (e.g., 시험, 회의, 여행, 수업, 사용). Examples are 바쁘신 중(에) 와 주셔서 감사합니다 'Thank you for coming when you are busy' and 회의 중(에) 전화가 왔어요 'There was a phone call in the middle of the meeting'.

윗사람 'senior, superior' vs. 아랫사람 'junior, subordinate'

윗사람에게 예의를 지키세요.

Please maintain proper etiquette with superiors.

우리 사장님은 **아랫사람**들에게 친절하세요.

Our CEO is kind to our employees.

▶ In Korean social groups, there are one's 윗사람 (*lit.* 'upper person') and 아랫사람 (*lit.* 'lower person'). In general, senior persons in terms of age (in social relations) or rank (in companies and government agencies) are 윗사람, while junior persons are 아랫사람.

저기요! 'Excuse me!' vs. 여기요! 'Excuse me!'

저기요!/여기요!, 여기 갈비탕 한 그릇하고 설렁탕 한 그릇 주세요.

Excuse me! Can we have one 갈비탕 and one 설렁탕?

▶ Both expressions are used to draw a person's attention, mainly a server in a restaurant. 저기요 'There!' is a hearer-oriented call although 저기 indicates a location away from both the speaker and hearer. 여기요 'Here!' is speaker-oriented.

GU6.11

~와/과(는) 달리/다르게 'unlike, differently from'

김 선생님**과(는) 달리/다르게** 이 선생님은 학생들을 특별히 잘 도와주신다.

Unlike Teacher Kim, Teacher Lee helps students particularly well.

예상**과 달리** 올해 경제가 좋아졌다.

The economy improved unexpectedly this year.

▶ The adverb 달리 is derived from the adjective 다르다 'be different' with the addition of the adverbializing suffix –리: 다르- + -리 → 달리. Similarly, the adverb 다르게 consists of 다르 plus the adverbializing suffix –게. 달리 and 다르게 obligatorily take the particle ~와/과 'with, from' and optionally the topic particle –는 when emphasis is called for.

GU6.12

~을/를 막론하고
'regardless of, irrespective of, not to speak of'

누구**를 막론하고** 이 사건과 관련된 사람은 다 조사할 것입니다.

No matter who they are, everyone involved in this case will be investigated.

어느 나라**를 막론하고** 잘사는 사람들과 못사는 사람들이 있어요.

Regardless which country it is, (in every country) there are rich and
poor people.

▶ 막론하다 'go without question, not discuss', where 막론 is a Sino-Korean bound noun meaning 'stopping discussion', is used only in the connective form 막론하고 and is always preceded by an object noun or pronoun with –을/를.

▶ Frequently used idiomatic expressions include 동서고금을 막론하고 'regardless of times and places' (*lit.* 'regardless of east or west, ancient or modern times'), 이유여하를 막론하고 'regardless of whatever reasons', and 지위고하를 막론하고 'regardless of (high or low) ranks'.

> **GU6.13**

~는/(으)ㄴ 반면(에)   'but on the other hand'

언니는 건강**한 반면(에)** 오빠는 건강이 별로 좋지 않아요.
My older sister is healthy, but my older brother, on the other hand, is not so healthy.

한국 사람들은 영어를 잘 읽고 이해하**는 반면(에)** 쓰고 말하는 것은 잘 못 하는 편이에요.
Koreans read and understand English well, but on the other hand they tend to be poor at writing and speaking.

▶ This pattern is used to juxtapose two contrasting states or actions. It is composed of the modifier ending –는/(으)ㄴ, its head noun 반면 'opposite side', and the particle 에 'at, on, in', which can be omitted without a change in meaning.

활동

가... 주어진 표현을 사용해서 다음 문장을 한국어로 바꾸어 보세요.

1. Nine out of ten people went to Korea. (~ 중(에서))

   _____.

2. Unlike Prof. Kim, Prof. Lee's class is easy. (~와/과(는) 달리)

   _____.

3. Regardless of country, politicians lie. (~을/를 막론하고)

   _____.

4. Jane sings well; on the other hand, she is not good at sports.   (반면에)

   _____.

나... 다음에 맞는 단어를 찾아서 써 주세요.

> 조화, 아랫사람, 개인주의, 민감하다, 대조적,
> 윗사람, 평등주의, 집단주의, 휴학, 계층주의

1. contrastive   _____.

2. harmony, balance   _____.

3. one's elder, one's superior   _____.

4. one's junior, one's subordinate   _____.

5. hierarchism   _____ .

6. collectivism   _____ .

7. egalitarianism   _____ .

8. individualism   _____ .

9. be sensitive   _____ .

10. taking time off from school   _____ .

다... 다음 표현을 친구한테 하는 말로 바꿔 보세요.

1. 안녕히 주무세요.   _____ .

2. 또 뵙겠습니다.   _____ .

3. 만나서 반갑습니다.   _____ .

4. 아침 드셨어요?   _____ .

5. 어디 가세요?   _____ .

라... 다음 대화를 읽고 아래 질문에 대답하세요.

> **대학교 동아리 '영화에 미쳤다' 신입생 환영회가 삼겹살 집에서 열렸다.**
>
> 김민준: 안녕하세요. 16학번 김민준이고요, 영문학과 2학년입니다. 동아리 '영화에 미쳤다' 회장을 맡고 있습니다. 만나서 반갑습니다. 그럼, 오늘 처음 만났으니까 자기 소개부터 시작할까요? 선배들이 먼저 소개하고 그 다음에 신입생들이 하죠. 이름이랑 학번, 전공 정도 말씀해 주세요.

이민호: 안녕하세요. 이민호입니다. 저는 재수해서 16학번이고요, 지금 경제학을 공부하고 있습니다. 우리 동아리에서는 홍보를 담당하고 있습니다. 후배 여러분, 만나서 반갑습니다.

박지호: 안녕하세요. 박지호입니다. 저는 14학번인데, 군대를 갔다 와서 지금은 2학년입니다. 전공은 전자공학입니다. 반갑습니다.

차수빈: 안녕하세요. 16학번 최수빈입니다. 제가 좀 나이 들어 보이는데, 재수, 삼수 아닙니다. 여기 회장하고 동갑이거든요. '영화에 미쳤다'에서 총무를 맡고 있습니다.

김민준: 자! 선배들 인사는 끝났고, 그럼 이제 우리 신입생들 소개해 주시죠.

이민지: 안녕하세요. 처음 뵙겠습니다. 17학번 이민지입니다. 전공은 아직 안 정했고요. 영화를 너무 너무 좋아해서 이 동아리에 들어왔습니다. 잘 부탁드립니다.

최민우: 안녕하세요. 제가 여기서 가장 어린 것 같은데요, 빠른 99년생, 17학번 최민우입니다. 저는 영화는 잘 모르는데요, 제 친구 민지 따라서 이 동아리에 왔습니다.

이준기: 안녕하세요. 이준기입니다. 저는 삼수해서 16학번이고요, 나이는 많지만 선배님들, 후배님들하고 잘 지내고 싶습니다. '영화에 미쳤다' 파이팅!

김민준: 네, 신입생 여러분, 진심으로 환영합니다. 다들 앞에 잔 채우시고 건배 한번 하지요. 건배!!!!

삼겹살 pork belly meat 신입생 new student 환영회 welcoming party 영문학과 English (Literature) Department 회장 president, chairman 맡다 to take charge 재수하다 to study for the second try to enter a college 홍보 PR 담당하다 to be in charge of 군대 army, military 전자공학 electrical engineering 나이 들다 to get old 삼수 third try for college entrance exam 동갑 same age 총무 manager 진심으로 truly 채우다 to fill 건배 cheers

1. 위의 자기 소개에서 어떤 호칭어가 나왔습니까?

2. 서로를 어떻게 부르면 좋을지 생각해 보세요.

김민준 ⇔ 차수빈

김민준 ⇔ 이민호

이민지 ⇔ 최민우

김민준 ⇔ 이준기

김민준 ⇔ 박지호

3. 여러분 반 학생들도 돌아가면서 동아리 회원들처럼 자기 소개를 하고 학년, 전공, 취미를 발표하세요. 그리고 한국어로 서로가 어떻게 호칭해야 할 것인지 생각해 보세요.

마... 다음 속담은 인간관계를 나타내는 속담입니다. 무슨 뜻인지 생각해 봅시다.

1. "찬물도 위 아래가 있다."

2. "가는 말이 고와야 오는 말이 곱다."

3. "말 한마디로 천 냥 빚을 갚는다."

바... 호칭어 사용에서 한국어와 여러분 언어의 차이에 대해서 100자 정도의 글을
한국어로 써 보세요.

_____

_____

_____

_____

_____

_____

_____

_____

_____

친가와 외가

한국에서는 아버지 쪽의 친척과 어머니 쪽의 친척을 조금 다르게 부른다. 먼저 아버지의 아버지·어머니는 할아버지·할머니라고 부르며, 할아버지·할머니 댁을 친가라고 한다. 아버지의 형은 큰아버지, 큰아버지의 아내는 큰어머니라고 부른다. 아버지의 남동생은 결혼하기 전에는 삼촌이라고 부르지만, 결혼을 한 후에는 작은아버지라고 부르고 작은아버지의 아내는 작은어머니라고 부른다. 아버지의 누나나 여동생은 고모라고 부르며 결혼을 하면 그 남편은 고모부라고 부른다. 큰아버지나 작은아버지의 자녀들은 사촌이라고 하는데 나이 차이와 성별에 따라 사촌 형, 사촌 누나, 사촌 오빠, 사촌 언니, 사촌 동생 등으로 지칭한다. 하지만 그들을 부를 때에는 그냥 형, 누나, 오빠, 언니로 호칭한다.

어머니 쪽의 친척을 지칭할 때는 "외"를 앞에 붙인다. 어머니의 아버지·어머니는 외할아버지·외할머니라고 하며, 외할아버지·외할머니 댁을 외가 또는 외갓집이라고 한다. 어머니의 남자 형제들은 외삼촌이라고 하며, 외삼촌이 결혼을 하면 아내를 외숙모라고 한다. 외삼촌의 자녀들은 외사촌이라고 하고 외사촌 형, 외사촌 오빠 등으로 지칭한다. 어머니의 언니나 여동생은 이모라고 부르며 이모가 결혼

친척 relative 차이 difference 성별 sex, gender 지칭하다 to call, refer to 호칭하다 to call, address 구별하다 to distinguish

을 해서 남편이 있으면 이모부라고 부른다. 외가의 친척들 중 '외-'자가 붙은 사람들을 호칭할 때에는 '외-' 없이 할아버지, 할머니, 삼촌, 숙모, 형, 오빠 등으로 부를 수 있다.

　이 밖의 친척들을 부르는 여러 호칭과 지칭들이 있지만 요즘에는 잘 쓰이지 않는다. 예전에는 친척들끼리 관계가 가깝고 만나는 일이 자주 있어서 서로 관계를 정확하게 구별할 수 있어야 했지만 요즘은 친척들을 만날 기회가 많이 없어졌기 때문에 친척들을 부를 일도 줄어들었기 때문이다.

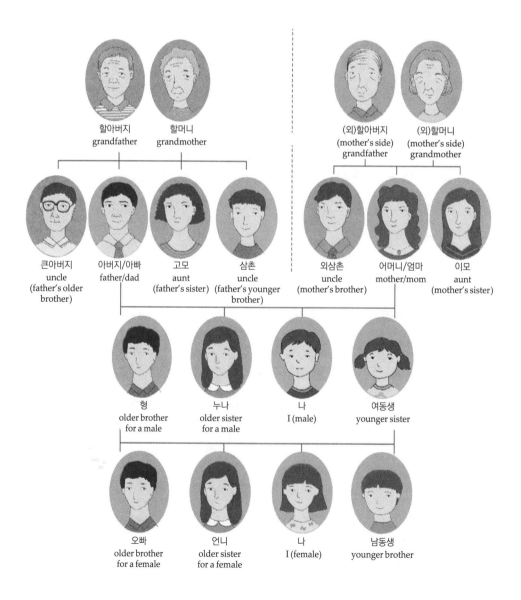

문 화

한국 회사의 직급

회사마다 조금씩 다르기는 하지만 대체로 다음 표와 같은 계층적인
직급이 있다. 그룹은 여러 회사를 자회사(daughter company)로 갖고
있는 재벌 그룹을 말한다. 예를 들면 삼성 그룹, 현대 그룹, LG 그룹
등은 각각 많은 자회사를 가지고 있다.

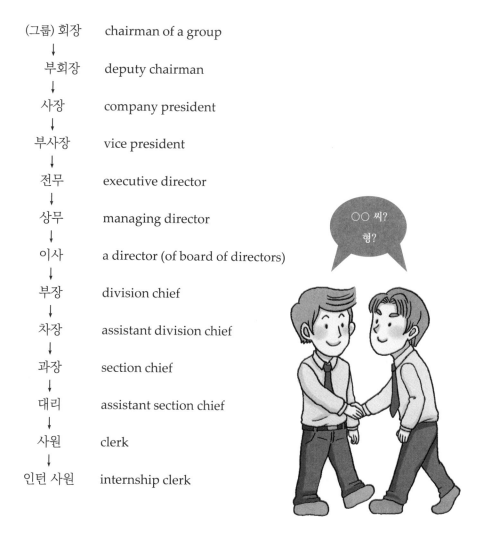

(그룹) 회장   chairman of a group
↓
부회장   deputy chairman
↓
사장   company president
↓
부사장   vice president
↓
전무   executive director
↓
상무   managing director
↓
이사   a director (of board of directors)
↓
부장   division chief
↓
차장   assistant division chief
↓
과장   section chief
↓
대리   assistant section chief
↓
사원   clerk
↓
인턴 사원   internship clerk

▰▰ 번역문 ▰▰

CONVERSATION:
Division Chief Kim and Assistant Section Chief Lee

Division Chief Chiho Kim and Assistant Section Chief Chun'gi Lee, both of whom work at a computer company, run into each other at a department store on a Sunday.

Assistant Section Chief Lee: (speaking to Division Chief Kim who is looking at women's clothing) Division Chief, Hello.

Division Chief Kim: Ah, Assistant Section Chief Lee, what brought you here?

Lee: Our kid says he's going to Mt. Dobong with friends, so I'm thinking about buying him a pair of hiking shoes.

Hey Minho, say hello. He's the Division Chief at my company.

Minho: Hello!

Kim: Hi Minho. You are very handsome!

You look just like your dad. So what year in school are you?

Minho: I'm a third grader in elementary school.

Lee: So what brought you here, Division Chief?

Kim: I'm thinking of buying and sending a couple pieces of winter clothes to my daughter in Chicago, since my wife says she's going to go visit her soon.

Ah, here's my wife coming this way!

Honey, this is Assistant Section Chief Chun'gi Lee from work. He's a very talented person. He says he's here to buy his son hiking shoes.

Lee: Madam, it's nice to meet you (*lit.* This is my first time meeting you). I'm Chun'gi Lee. I work under Division Chief Kim.

Mrs. Kim: It's nice to meet you, Assistant Section Chief Lee.

Your son is very cute.

He really takes after his father.

Lee: That's what everyone says (*lit.* Everyone says that).

Kim: Well I'm sure you're busy, so why don't you go and take a look at some hiking shoes right away. Assistant Section Chief Lee, it was nice seeing you.

Lee: Yes, I'll do that.

Please excuse me leaving first (*lit.* I will do a discourtesy first).

Minho, let's go.

Minho: Yes, dad.

(to Division Chief Kim and his wife) Goodbye.

Kim & Mrs. Kim: Bye, Minho.

(a moment later)

Lee: Ah, over there, Ms. Subin Ch'a is coming this way, too!

Ms. Subin Ch'a!

Ch'a: Oh my, how are you, Assistant Section Chief Lee?

Lee: I guess you are here for shopping.

Ch'a: That's right. I came with my friends to buy some things.

Lee: Well enjoy your shopping. I will see you at work tomorrow.

Ch'a: Alright, see you tomorrow.

READING: The Culture of Korean Address Terms

In everyday conversation, there is a need for language etiquette. One aspect of language etiquette is the method by which one refers to the other party in conversation. The term for how the other party is addressed is *hoch'ing-ŏ* (address term), and when compared to English, Korean address terms are considerably more complex and there are a wider variety of address terms. The use of address terms, along with honorifics, is one of the most sensitive aspects of language etiquette in interpersonal relations. Address terms display the relationship between the speaker and the listener. Using the proper address term helps the conversation go smoothly, and it helps the relationship between the people in the conversation.

Address terms can be divided into two main groups: kinship terms and non-kin terms. Kinship terms include address terms such as *abŏji* (father), *ŏmŏni* (mother), *hyŏng* (male's elder brother), and *ŏnni* (female's elder sister). Terms for calling one's daughter-in-law include *saeaga* (new child) and *ŏmŏm-a* (child's mom), while one may call her husband *oppa* (female's elder brother), *appa* (dad), *yŏbo* (honey), or [child's name] *appa*.

One of the characteristics of Korean society is that kinship terms are also used with people who are not family. This is done in order to express one's closeness with the person being addressed. One can refer to their friend's parents as "father" and "mother" and can call their seniors at school *hyŏng* or *ŏnni*. On the other hand, these terms are also used as sales tactics. At department stores and restaurants, employees may use terms such as "*abŏ-nim, ŏmŏ-nim, ŏnni*" (*hon*. father, *hon*. mother, elder sister) to attract customers' interests. Customers also usually call female employees either *ŏnni* or *imo* (maternal aunt).

There are a wide variety of non-kin address terms. To address someone who is not close or who is a superior, terms like *sŏnsaeng-nim* (teacher), *kyosu-nim* (professor), and *sajang-nim* (company president) are widely used. These terms combine a job title with the honorific title suffix -*nim*. They can also be used by placing the person's name before the address term, such as Kim (Yŏngsu) *sŏnsaeng-nim*. It is common to refer to one's senior at school or work using the term for senior *sŏnbae(-nim)*. The name can also be placed in front of this term, such as in Kim *sŏnbae(-nim)*. When addressing a child, their name can be used such as in *Hijŏng-a* and *Sumi-ya*, where a name ending with a consonant has -*a* attached, and a name ending with a vowel has -*ya* attached. Outside of these terms, there are address terms that can be used when the other party's name or job title is unknown. Depending on the age of the other party or the situation, these terms can include *haksaeng* (student), *chŏgi-yo* (there), *yŏgi-yo* (here), *son-nim* (guest), and *kogaeng-nim* (customer).

Unlike Korean, in English, people often shorten names in everyday conversation regardless of age or gender. If one's name is "Timothy Smith" he can be addressed as "Tim", and if one's name is "Christine Haig" she can be called "Chris". Shortening a name this way can help maintain a close relationship. Thus, many people will request that others call them by their nickname (shortened first name) during conversation.

While English speakers keep order within the (values of) equality and individualism, Korean people tend to maintain harmony through a certain degree of hierarchism and collectivism. Such contrasting culture exists in the background of Korean address terms, and the use of address terms has become more complicated in interpersonal relationships compared to the usage in English address terms. Because of such interpersonal relationships among Korean people, the Korean honorific system has developed as well.

FURTHER READING:
Relatives on One's Father's Side and Mother's Side

In Korea, people refer to the relatives on one's father's side and the relatives on one's mother's side somewhat differently. First, people call the father and mother of one's father *harabŏji* and *halmŏni*, and call the home of the paternal grandfather and grandmother, *ch'in'ga* (*lit*. close family). People call the elder brother of one's father *k'ŭn-abŏji* (*lit*. big father), and call the wife of the uncle, *k'ŭn-ŏmŏni* (*lit*. big mother). People call the younger brother of one's father *samch'on* (*lit*. third-removed) until the uncle gets married. Then they call him *chakŭn-abŏji* (*lit*. little father) when he marries, and people call the wife of the uncle, *chakŭn-ŏmŏni* (*lit*. little mother). People call the elder or younger sister of one's father *komo* (*lit*. aunt), then when a *komo* gets married, they call her husband *komobu* (*lit*. the husband of the aunt). People call the children of one's uncles (e.g., *k'ŭn-abŏji* or *chakŭn-abŏji*) *sach'on* (*lit*. fourth-removed, English equivalent of cousins). Depending on the age gap and gender, people refer to them as *sach'on hyŏng* (*lit*. fourth-removed elder brother to a male, an English equivalent of an elder male cousin to a male), *sach'on nuna* (*lit*. fourth-removed elder sister to a male, an English equivalent of an elder female cousin to a male), *sach'on oppa*, (*lit*. fourth-removed elder brother to a female, an English equivalent of an elder male cousin to a female), *sach'on ŏnni* (*lit*. fourth-removed elder sister to a female, an English equivalent of an older female cousin to a female), *sach'on tongsaeng* (*lit*. fourth-removed younger sibling; an English equivalent of a younger cousin), etc. However, when calling them, people just refer to them as *hyŏng* (an elder brother to a male), *nuna* (an elder sister to a male), *oppa* (an elder brother to a female), and *ŏnni* (an elder sister to a female).

When referring to the relatives on one's mother's side, people attach the prefix *oe-* (*lit*. outside) in front of the address titles. People call father and mother of one's mother *oe-harabŏji* (*lit*. outside grandfather) and *oe-halmŏni* (*lit*. outside grandmother, an English equivalent of maternal grandmother). They call the home of the maternal grandfather and grandmother *oega* or *oegatchip* (*lit.* outside home). People call brothers of one's mother *oe-samch'on* (*lit.* outside third-removed), and his wife *oe-sungmo* (*lit.* outside aunt) when the uncle marries. They refer to the uncle's children as *oe-sach'on*, such as *oe-sach'on hyŏng*, or *oe-sach'on oppa* (*lit.* outside fourth-removed elder brother). People call mother's elder or younger sister *imo* (aunt). When the aunt marries, they call the husband *imobu* (uncle). When calling maternal relatives, one can call them without adding the prefix '*oe-*' such as *haraboji* (grandfather), *halmŏni* (grandmother), *samch'on* (uncle), *sungmo* (aunt), *hyŏng* (an elder brother to a male), *oppa* (an elder brother to a female), etc.

In addition, there are address and referring terms that were used to call other relatives. In the past, relatives were close to each other and met frequently, so it was necessary to be able to accurately distinguish their relationships. However nowadays, there are fewer opportunities to meet relatives, thus fewer opportunities to address (*lit.* call) the relatives. This is the reason why various address terms are not frequently used these days.

CULTURE: Ranks in Korean Companies

Although each company is slightly different, there are generally hierarchical positions as shown in the diagram. A *kŭrup* refers to a chaebol group that has several companies as daughter companies. For example, Samsung Group, Hyundai Group, and LG Corp., etc. each has many daughter companies.

■■ 단어 ■■

가치관	values	며느리	daughter-in-law
간호사	nurse	모시다	to accompany; serve under
개인주의	individualism		
건배	cheers	모음	vowel
계층주의	hierarchism	뭐(=뭣)	something
고객	customer	민감하다	to be sensitive
과장	section chief	부르다	to call
관계	relationship	부사장	vice president of a company
구별하다	to distinguish		
구조	structure	부장	division chief
군대	army, military	부회장	vice president, vice chairman
그러겠다 =그렇게 하겠다	will do so		
		붙이다	to attach
기회	opportunity	비친족어	non-kin terms
나이 들다	to get old	사모님	one's teacher's or senior's wife
남	male		
남녀노소	men and women of all ages	사용법	usage
		사원	clerk
남편	husband	사장	company president
담당하다	to be in charge of	삼수	third try for college entrance exam
대리	assistant section chief		
대인 관계	interpersonal relations	상당히	considerably
대조적	contrastive	상대방	the other party
동갑	same age	상무	managing director
두어	a couple of	상업 전략	sales tactic
등산화	hiking shoes	상황	situation
딸애 = 딸아이	daughter	성명	full name
마음을 끌다	to attract, allure	성별	sex, gender
마주치다	to come across	순조롭다	to be smooth
맡다	to take charge	신입생	new student

실례하다	to be excused	존대법	honorifics
아내	wife	줄이다	to reduce
아드님	(honorific form of 아들)	지칭어	reference terms
어머	(feminine exclamation) Oh, my!	지칭하다	to call, refer to
		직원	clerk, employee
어서	quickly, please	직함	job title
언어 예절	language etiquette	진심으로	truly
영문학과	English Literature Department	질서	(social) order
		집단주의	collectivism
유능하다	to be competent	집사람	my wife
유지하다	to maintain	차이	difference
이모	aunt (mom's sister)	차장	assistant division chief
이사	director (of board of directors)	채우다	to fill
		총무	manager
인간관계	human relations	친밀함	intimacy
인사 드리다	to greet a senior	친족어	kinship terms
자녀	children, sons and daughters	친척	relative
		켤레	a pair (of hand and foot wear)
자음	consonant		
잠시 후	after a while	평등주의	egalitarianism
재수하다	to study for the second try to enter a college	호칭어	address terms
		호칭하다	to call, address
적절하다	to be appropriate	홍보	PR
전무	executive director	환영회	welcoming party
전자공학	electrical engineering	환자	patient
점원	clerk of a store	회장	president, chairman
조화	harmony		

유명한 한국의 인물

Lesson 7 Famous Korean People

학습 목표

내용 • 인물에 대해서 설명할 때 필요한 단어와 표현들을 익힌다.

문화 • 여러 분야에서 유명한 한국인들과 그들의 업적에 대해서
         알아본다.
      • 한국 역사상 중요한 인물들에 대해서 살펴본다.

인물 figure, person 분야 area, field 업적 achievement 역사상 historically, in history

■ 생각해 봅시다

가 ▸▸ 여러분이 가장 존경하는 유명한 사람의 이름, 업적, 존경하는 이유 등에
　 대해 이야기해 봅시다.

나 ▸▸ 다음 한국 사람들에 대해서 들어 본 적이 있습니까? 어떤 사람들인지
　 아는 대로 이야기해 봅시다.

강수진_발레리나
박지성_축구 선수
싸이_가수
박찬욱_영화 감독
반기문_전 UN사무총장
박인비_골프 선수
김연아_피겨 스케이트 선수
백남준_비디오 아티스트

다 ▸▸ 이 사람들 이외에 유명한 한국 사람들에 대해서 알아보고 이야기해
봅시다.

라 ▸▸ 다음은 한국 돈에 나오는 인물들입니다. 다음 사람들에 대해서 알아보고
여러분 나라의 돈에는 어떤 인물들이 나오는지 이야기해 봅시다.

신사임당

세종 대왕

율곡 이이

퇴계 이황

이순신 장군

한글과 한국어

선생님 연구실에서

선생님: 한국어 공부 재미있어요?

스티브: 네, 그런데 배우면 배울수록 어려운 것 같아요.

선생님: 음… 뭐가 제일 어려워요?

스티브: **뭐,**^{GU7.1} 한국어 발음이나 문법도 어렵고 존댓말도 아직 어려워요.

선생님: 계속 연습하**다 보면**^{GU7.2} 금방 한국어를 잘할 수 있을 거예요. 스티브 씨는 한국어 공부 잘 하고 있으니까 걱정 안 해도 돼요.

스티브: 세종 대왕이 한국어를 어렵게 만드신 것 같아요.

선생님: 아, 세종 대왕은 한글을 **만드셨지**^{GU7.3} 한국어를 만드신 건 아니에요.

스티브: 네? 세종 대왕이 한글을 만드셔서 한국 사람들이 한국어를 사용하게 **된 거 아니에요?** ^{GU7.4}

선생님: 그러니까 그게, 언어와 문자가 같은 것은 아니잖아요?

스티브: 음… 그렇죠.

선생님: 한글이 없던 옛날에도 한국 사람들은 한국어로 말했지만 예전에는 문자가 없었던 거죠.

스티브: 아…

선생님: 그런데 세종 대왕이 한국어를 위한 문자를 만드신 거예요. 그

발음 pronunciation 문법 grammar 문자 letter, character 글 (a piece of) writing

게 1446년이니까 지금부터 600년쯤 전이네요.

스티브: 그렇군요. 그럼 한글이 없었을 때에는 사람들이 어떻게 글을 썼지요?

선생님: 한자로 글을 썼어요. 쉽게 말하자면 이야기할 때에는 한국어로 했지만 글로 쓸 때에는 뜻에 따라서 한자로 쓴 것이지요.

스티브: 그럼 사람들이 한자를 쓸 줄 알았나요?

선생님: 아니요. 대부분의 사람들은 교육을 받을 기회가 없어서 글을 쓰거나 읽을 수가 없었어요. 조선 시대에는 양반이라는 귀족 계급이 있었는데 그 양반들**이나**$^{GU7.5}$ 읽고 쓸 수 있었지요.

스티브: 그럼 많은 사람들이 읽고 쓸 수 없었겠네요?

선생님: 그렇죠. 대부분의 사람들이 교육을 받을 수 없었어요. 이것을 안타깝게 생각한 세종 대왕이 직접 한글을 만드신 거예요.

스티브: 왕이 직접 만들었**다고요?** $^{GU7.6}$

선생님: 네, 세종 대왕은 어릴 때부터 총명하고 공부를 많이 해서 훌륭한 학자였다고 해요.

스티브: 와, 정말 대단한 왕이네요!

선생님: 한글뿐만 아니라 세종 대왕은 과학, 경제, 국방, 예술, 문화 등 여러 분야에서 많은 업적을 남기셔서 한국 역사상 가장 훌륭한 왕이라고 사람들이 생각해요. 만 원짜리 지폐에도 세종 대왕이 있잖아요.

스티브: 그래서 광화문에 세종 대왕 동상도 있군요.

선생님: 이제 한글에 대해서 확실히 알겠지요?

스티브: 네, 그리고 세종 대왕에 대해서도 많이 알게 됐어요.

쉽게 말하자면 to put it plainly 양반 aristocratic class of the Chosǒn Dynasty 귀족 계급 noble class 안타깝다 to be regrettable, pitiful 총명하다 to be brilliant 훌륭하다 to be excellent, splendid 학자 scholar 대단하다 to be incredible 국방 national defense 예술 art 지폐 bill, paper money 광화문 Gwanghwamun Gate 동상 statue 확실히 clearly

이해 문제

가... 다음 내용이 대화의 내용과 같으면 ○, 다르면 X에 표시하세요.

1. 세종 대왕은 한국어를 만들었다.   ○   X

2. 옛날에는 대부분의 사람들은 글을 쓸 수 없었다.   ○   X

3. 세종 대왕은 사람들에게 한자를 가르치고 싶어 하셨다.   ○   X

4. 세종 대왕은 훌륭한 학자였다.   ○   X

5. 한국 사람들은 세종 대왕을 존경한다.   ○   X

나... 다음 질문에 대답해 보세요.

1. 세종 대왕의 업적은 어떤 것들이 있습니까?

2. 한글이 없을 때에 사람들은 어떻게 글을 썼습니까?

3. 조선 시대의 많은 사람들은 왜 읽고 쓸 수 없었습니까?

4. 한국 사람들이 세종 대왕을 존경하는 이유는 무엇입니까?

문법과 용법

뭐   (oh,) well

가: 요즘 어떻게 지내세요?

How are you these days?

나: **뭐**, 좀 바쁘게 지내고 있어요.

Well, I am a little busy.

가: 오늘 시간 있어요?

Do you have time today?

나: 오늘은 바쁜데요.

I am busy today.

가: **뭐**, 그럴 줄 알았어요.

Oh well, I expected that.

▶ 뭐 is a contracted form of the question pronoun 무어 or 무엇 'what'. It functions as a so-called discourse particle or an exclamatory expression with the meaning of 'well!', 'what!', 'why!', or 'what else'. 뭐 can be used in the beginning of a statement to express a casual attitude on what the speaker is going to say. Depending on the context and/or your tone of voice, it can be sometimes used to express slight reproach to the listener about what was just said. At the end of a statement, it means 'what else', as in 나는 날마다 놀지요, 뭐 'I play around every day, what else?'

~다(가) 보면
'if/when one does over a period of time'

열심히 노력하**다가 보면** 꼭 성공할 거예요.

If you keep making an effort, you will definitely succeed.

살**다 보면** 여러 가지 일들이 있어요.

As you go through life, you will encounter many things.

이렇게 술만 마시**다 보면** 건강이 나빠질 거예요.

If you keep drinking like this, your health will deteriorate.

▶ This pattern is used after a verb or adjective stem to mean that "if one does something or is in a state over a period of time, then (she/he will discover some result)". It combines the "transferring" connective ending –다(가) 'stop doing, while doing' with the verb stem 보 'see' and the "conditional" connective ending –면.

~지 'and/but [opposite meaning]'

저 분은 키만 컸**지** 힘은 약해요.

That person may be tall, but he is weak.

저는 여기 직원이**지** 사장이 아니에요.

I am an employee here, not the president.

▶ The connective ending –지 'and, but' is used to emphasize two contrasting facts or events. Its meaning is similar to the conjunctive ending –지만 'but'. This begs the question of whether it has developed from the latter via contraction.

> GU7.4
>
> ## ~는/(으)ㄴ/(으)ㄹ 거 아니에요?   'Isn't it that ...?'

저 두 사람 헤어**진 거 아니었어요?**

Didn't those two break up?

오늘 숙제 없**는 거 아니었어요?**

Didn't we not have homework today?

여름에 한국 가**실 거 아니에요?**

Aren't you going to Korea this summer?

▶ Following a modifier clause, this pattern is used to confirm the fact given in the modifier clause that the speaker thought correct but seemingly not. Sometimes, it is used to express one's surprise because something appears to be different from what she/he has assumed. The bound noun 거 in the pattern is a contraction of 것 'thing, fact'.

GU7.5

~(이)나 'just; (at least) something or the like; or something like that'

이런 책은 초등학생들**이나** 보는 책이에요.

This kind of book is for elementary students or something.

오늘은 집에서 잠**이나** 자야겠어요.

I will just sleep at home today.

커피**나** 마실까요?

Shall we drink some coffee or something?

▶ The particle (이)나 is multifunctional with several different meanings: 1. 'or' as in 미아나 톰이 온다 'Mia or Tom will come', 2. 'about, as much as' as in 10만 원이나 벌 었어요 'I earned as much as 10,000 won', 몇 개나 살까요? 'About how many should we buy?', 3. 'any/every– ' as in 이 은행의 ATM은 미국 어디에나 있어요 'ATMs for this bank can be found anywhere in the U.S.', and 4. 'just, or something' as in the present pattern. In the last function, (이)나 marks the noun it follows as a possible option, but one that is not necessarily first choice.

GU7.6

~고(요)? 'Did you say that ...?'

가: 지금 영화 보러 갈까?

　　Shall we go to see a movie now?

나: 영화 보러 가자**고?** 내일 시험이잖아!

Go to see a movie? We have a test tomorrow!

가: 저 내일 한국에 가요.

I am going to Korea tomorrow.

나: 한국에 가신다**고요?** 갑자기 왜요?

Going to Korea? Why all of a sudden?

▶ This echo-question ending is mostly used in casual conversation when the speaker wants to ask for clarification about what he/she just heard or something is hard to believe. This is basically the indirect quotation of what the speaker just heard. Thus, indirect quotation rules of conjugation apply here, as in 간다고요?, 갔다고요?, 가냐고요?, 갔냐고요?, 가라고요?, 가자고요?, 좋다고요?, 좋았다고요?, 좋냐고요?, 좋았냐고요?, 학생이라고요?, 학생이었다고요?, 학생이냐고요?, 학생이었냐고요?, etc.

가... 아래 영어 문장의 뜻에 맞게 보기에서 적당한 표현을 골라서 문장을 완성하세요.

> ~(으)ㄴ/는/(으)ㄹ 거 아니에요?, (이)나, ~다(가) 보면, ~고요?, ~지

1. Aren't these shoes too big for you?

이 신발 너무 _____?

2. If you keep studying hard, you will definitely pass the exam.

열심히 _____ 시험에 붙을 거예요.

3. Only the exterior of the building is good, the inside is very old.

저 건물은 겉모습만 _____ 안은 아주 오래됐어요.

4. Shall we go hiking or something?

우리 등산 _____ 갈까요?

5. You have a cold? Go home and get some rest.

감기에 _____? 집에 가서 좀 쉬세요.

나... 보기에서 가장 적당한 말을 골라 빈칸을 채우세요. 각 단어를 한 번씩만 쓰세요.

> 직접, 아직, 대부분, 아마, 확실히

1. ㄱ: 한국어 공부 어때요?

   ㄴ: 한국어를 3년이나 배웠는데 _____ 어려워요.

2. ㄱ: 한국어 반 학생들의 90%는 한국에서 공부한 적이 있어요.

   ㄴ: 와, 학생들이 _____ 한국에 갔다 왔군요!

3. ㄱ: 이 이야기는 전화로 얘기하는 것보다 _____ 만나서 얘기를
   하는 게 좋을 것 같아.

   ㄴ: 그래 그럼. 내일 몇 시에 만날까?

4. ㄱ: 어제 수업에서 배운 문법 잘 알겠어요?

   ㄴ: 네, 열심히 공부해서 이제는 _____ 알아요.

5. ㄱ: 내일 날씨가 어떨까요?

   ㄴ: 구름이 많은 것을 보니까 _____ 비가 올 것 같아요.

다... 다음 밑줄 친 단어와 가장 비슷한 뜻의 단어를 찾으세요.

1. 토머스 에디슨이 어렸을 때부터 총명했던 것은 아니다.

   ㄱ. 똑똑했던   ㄴ. 훌륭했던   ㄷ. 뚱뚱했던   ㄹ. 기억했던

2. 선생님께서는 요리 솜씨가 <u>대단하세요.</u>

   ㄱ. 크세요   ㄴ. 보통이세요   ㄷ. 중요하세요   ㄹ. 훌륭하세요

3. <u>예전</u>에는 컴퓨터가 아주 크고 비쌌는데 요즘에는 작고 싸졌어요.

   ㄱ. 옛날   ㄴ. 이따가   ㄷ. 그때   ㄹ. 현대

4. 여러 나라의 <u>언어</u>를 배우면 여행할 때 편리할 거예요.

   ㄱ. 문법   ㄴ. 말씀   ㄷ. 표현   ㄹ. 말

5. 한국어로 이야기 할 때에는 <u>존댓말</u>을 잘 써야 해요.

   ㄱ. 인사말   ㄴ. 반말   ㄷ. 높임말   ㄹ. 거짓말

라... 세종 대왕 이외에 한국 사람들이 존경하는 역사적 인물에는 어떤 사람들이 있는지 알아보고 그중에서 한 사람에 대해 소개하는 글을 써 봅시다.

마... 여러분 나라 사람들이 존경하는 역사적 인물에는 어떤 사람들이 있는지 이야기 해 보고 그중에서 한 사람을 골라 소개하는 글을 써 봅시다.

비디오 아티스트 백남준

한국계 현대 예술가 중 세계에서 제일 유명한 사람은 아마 백남준 (Nam June Paik)일 것이다. 백남준은 텔레비전, 카메라, 비디오 등을 통해 표현하는 예술인 비디오아트를 처음 만들고 발전시킨 사람이다. 그는 1932년에 한국에서 유복한 가정에서 태어나 초등학교와 중학교 때는 피아노와 작곡을 배웠다. 고등학교는 홍콩에서 다녔고 그 후에 일본 도쿄대학에서 미술사 및^GU7.7 음악사를 전공했다. 졸업 후에 독일로 유학을 떠나 서양의 건축, 음악사, 철학 등을 공부했다.

그는 독일에서 여러 음악가들과 함께 예술 퍼포먼스 활동을 하며 유명해졌고 이때 텔레비전과 비디오를 이용하여 비디오아트 실험을 했다. 이후 미국 뉴욕으로 활동 무대를 옮겨 세계적인 비디오아트 예술가로 알려졌다. 1984년 1월 1일에는 세계의 유명한 예술가들의 퍼포먼스를 인공위성을 통해 방송한 "굿모닝 미스터 오웰"(Good Morning, Mr. Orwell)이라는 프로그램을 기획하여 세계인들의 **관심을 모았다.**^GU7.8 대표작으로는 "달은 가장 오래된 TV"(Moon is the Oldest TV) "TV부처"(TV-Buddha) "TV 첼로"(TV Cello) "다다익선"(The More

---

한국계 Korean descent 현대 modern 예술가 artist 표현하다 to express 발전시키다 to foster, develop 유복하다 to be affluent 가정 family, home 작곡 musical composition 미술사 art history 유학 study abroad 떠나다 to leave 건축 architecture 음악사 history of music 철학 philosophy 실험 experiment 활동 무대 one's field of action 인공위성 satellite 기획하다 to plan

the Better) 등이 있다.

　1990년대 중반까지 활발하게 작품 활동을 하던 백남준은 1995년 뇌졸중으로 쓰러지고 2006년에 미국 마이애미의 자택에서 **별세했다.**^{GU7.9} 백남준의 여러 작품들은 세계의 유명한 미술관에서 많은 사람들의 사랑을 받고 있다.

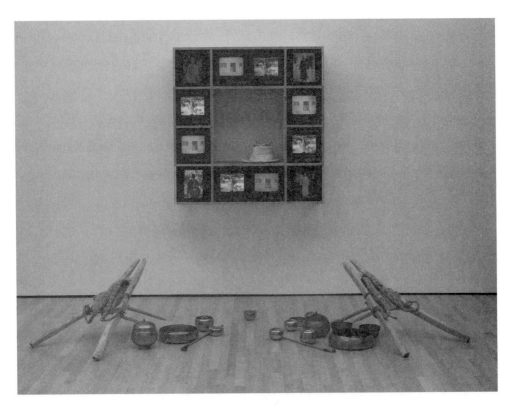

"Chongro Cross", 1991.

뇌졸중 a stroke　자택 one's own home　작품 work (of art)　별세하다 to depart this life

읽기 2

피겨스케이팅 선수 김연아

2014년 러시아 소치 겨울 올림픽이 끝나고, 피겨스케이팅 선수 김연아는 은퇴했다. 그래도 김연아는 여전히 세계적인 스타이고 '국민 영웅'이다. 은반을 떠났지만 아직도 한국인들은 김연아를 그리워한다. 다음은 김연아 선수와의 인터뷰이다.

기자: "가장 매력적인 한국인"을 뽑는 설문 조사에서 김연아 선수가 1등으로 뽑혔는데 그 이유가 뭐라고 생각하시는지요GU7.10?

김연아: 사실 피겨스케이팅이 그동안 한국에서는 주목받지 못했던 것 같아요. 그런데 제가 외국 선수들과 경쟁해서 자주 이겼으니까 예쁘게 봐 주신 것 같습니다.

기자: 은퇴한 뒤 그동안 어떻게 지내셨는지요?

김연아: 선수 때는 일주일에 5~6일 훈련하면서 늘 바쁘게 살았어요. 은퇴한 뒤에는 훈련을 하지 않아도 되고, 부상에 대한 걱정을 안 해도 돼서 좋습니다. 그리고 앞으로 여유가 생기면 여행을 많이 하고 싶어요.

선수 player 은퇴하다 to retire 국민 (people of a) nation 영웅 hero 은반 ice rink (*lit.* silver plate) 그리워하다 to miss, long for 기자 reporter 매력적이다 to be attractive, charming 이기다 to win 부상 injury 여유 free (time)

기자: 피겨스케이팅 선수 생활을 돌이켜 보면 어떠세요?

김연아: 선수 생활을 하면서 너무 많은 아픔이 있었어요. **수백**
^{GU7.11} 번, 수천 번 넘어지면서 정말 많이 다쳤어요. 포
기하고 싶은 순간도 많았고요. 그래도 아팠던 순간이
있었기 때문에 더 성숙해질 수 있었다고 생각해요.

김연아는 마지막으로 "오랜 시간이 지나도 '피겨퀸' '은반 위의 여
왕'으로 오랫동안 기억되고 싶습니다"**라고 전했다**.^{GU7.11}

[출처: 중앙일보 은퇴 19개월 '은반의 여왕' 김연아 인터뷰]

돌이켜 보다 to look back 아픔 pain 포기하다 to give up 성숙해지다 to become mature
여왕 queen 기억되다 to be remembered 전하다 to tell, convey

이해 문제

가... 다음 내용이 본문의 내용과 같으면 ○, 다르면 X에 표시하세요.

(읽기 1)

1. 백남준은 어렸을 때 가난한 집에서 자랐다.　　　　　　○　　X

2. 백남준은 고등학교 때부터 외국 유학을 했다.　　　　　○　　X

3. 백남준은 일본에서 비디오아트를 공부했다.　　　　　○　　X

(읽기 2)

1. 김연아는 이제 피겨스케이트 선수가 아니다.　　　　　○　　X

2. 김연아는 그동안 여행을 많이 했다.　　　　　　　　○　　X

3. 김연아는 피겨스케이트 선수였을 때 포기한 적이 있다.　○　　X

나... 다음 질문에 대답해 보세요.

1. 백남준은 대학교에서 무엇을 전공했습니까?

2. 백남준은 언제부터 세계적인 예술가로 알려졌습니까?

3. "굿모닝 미스터 오웰"은 어떤 작품입니까?

4. 김연아가 선수였을 때 제일 힘들었던 것은 무엇입니까?

5. 김연아는 은퇴한 이후에 어떻게 지내고 있습니까?

6. 김연아가 "매력적인 한국인"으로 뽑힌 이유는 무엇인지 써 봅시다.

문법과 용법

및 'and, as well as'

이 서류에 주소 **및** 전화번호를 적어 주세요.

Please write your address and telephone number on this form.

이 가수들은 한국 **및** 세계 여러 나라에서 인기가 많아요.

These singers are famous in Korea as well as in many other countries around the world.

▶ The connective adverb 및 is a formal or written equivalent of the connective particles 과/와 or connective adverb 그리고 or 또한. Sometimes, it is used along with other connectives, as in 노래와 춤 및 사랑 'song, dance, and love'.

관심을 모으다/끌다/받다 = 주목을 받다/끌다 'get attention'

박지성은 고등학교 때부터 뛰어난 축구 실력으로 **주목을 받았다**.

Since high school, Ji-sung Park has received much attention for his excellent soccer skills.

한국 아이돌 그룹들은 더 많은 사람들의 **관심을 받으려고** 최선을 다한다.

Korean idol groups try their best to get more people's attention.

▶ There are many ways to express the concept of one getting attention. The relevant pattern combines the Sino-Korean noun 관심 'interest' or 주목 'attention' and the verb 받다 'receive' and 끌다 'draw'. 관심 also occurs with 모으다 'collect'.

GU7.9

별세(하다) 'depart this life, pass away'

그는 할머니의 **별세** 소식을 듣고 바로 고향으로 갔다.

Upon hearing of his grandmother's passing, he went directly to his home-town.

2016년 6월 27일에 유명한 미래학자 앨빈 토플러가 87세의 나이로 **별세했**습니다.

On June 27th, 2016, Alvin Toffler, a famous futurist, died at 87.

▶ The non-honorific verb for 'die' is the native word 죽다, which is used for humans, animals, plants, and, metaphorically, for inanimate objects and concepts. The Sino-Korean non-honorific noun 사망 'death' and verb 사망하다 are used only for humans, especially in writing, reports, and formal speech. On the other hand, euphemistic expressions are used to refer to senior persons' death. The native verb is 돌아가시다 'turn around and go', while the Sino-Korean noun is 별세 'depart the world' and the verb is 별세하다.

GU7.10

~(으)ㄴ/는지요? 'I am wondering if ...'

내일 바**쁜지요?**

I'm wondering if you are busy tomorrow?

요즘 어떻게 지내시**는지요?**

I'm wondering how are you these days?

▶ This question sentence ending is used to ask something indirectly, which gives a polite feeling. After an adjective or copula stem, ~(으)ㄴ지요? is used, while after a verb stem or the past form of , ~는지요? is used.

▶ This pattern has developed from the indirect question construction where 지 is a bound noun meaning 'whether, if'. Thus, for example, 밖에 비가 오는지 모르겠어요 'I wonder if it is raining outside' and 제니가 오는지 아세요? 'Do you know whether Jennie is coming?' are regular indirect question constructions. The pattern in question has derived by omitting the main clause in such constructions. ‒요 is attached to 지 if a polite level is called for.

GU7.11

수~ 'multiples of (the number)'

그는 **수십** 년 동안 노력해서 큰 부자가 되었다.

After decades of hard work, he became very wealthy.

수천 명의 사람들이 먹을 수 있는 음식들이 매일 버려지고 있습니다.

Every day, food that could have been eaten by thousands of people is thrown away.

▶ The basic meaning of the Sino-Korean noun 수 is 'number', as in 우리 학교의 학생 수는 1,000명이 넘어요 'The number of students in our school is more than 1,000'. 수 also means 'several, a few, a number of' as in 수일 동안 'for several days; for a few days', 수년 후에 'after several years; after a few years', 수십 'scores, tens', 수백 'hundreds', 수천 'thousands', 수만 'tens of thousands' 수없이 'countlessly'.

GU7.12

전하다 'convey, tell, deliver, hand (over)'

부모님께 감사하다고 **전해** 주세요.

Please convey my gratitude to your parents.

전하실 말씀 있으세요?

Do you have anything to tell me?

▶ The transitive verb 전하다 is composed of the Sino-Korean bound noun 전 'transmission' and the verb 하다 'do'. It can have an object noun such as 소식 'news', 말씀 'words', and 편지 'letter'. It can also have a reported clause in the form ~다고/라고 전하다, as in 나는 잘 있다고 전해 주세요 'Please tell them that I am doing fine' and 미아는 스무 살이라고 전해 주세요 'Please let them know that Mia is twenty years old'.

활동

가... 비슷한 뜻을 가진 단어나 표현과 연결해 보세요.

1. 돈이 많이 있다   •   • 그리워하다

2. 외국에서 공부를 하다   •   • 유복하다

3. 여러 사람들에게 알려지다 •   • 돌아가시다

4. 보고 싶어 하다   •   • 유학하다

5. 별세하다   •   • 유명하다

나... 빈칸에 가장 알맞은 말을 찾으세요.

1. 요즘 사람들은 주로 인터넷을 _____ 뉴스를 본다.

　ㄱ. 통해   ㄴ. 열고   ㄷ. 받아서   ㄹ. 해서

2. 이번 공연에서 가수들은 화려한 춤으로 사람들의 관심을 _____.

　ㄱ. 모았다   ㄴ. 보였다   ㄷ. 가졌다   ㄹ. 했다

3. 저 배우는 나이가 많지만 _____ 아름답다.

　ㄱ. 벌써   ㄴ. 곧   ㄷ. 여전히   ㄹ. 바로

4. 요즘 세계적으로 _____ 한국 가수들이 많아요.

　ㄱ. 유행한   ㄴ. 알리는   ㄷ. 모르는   ㄹ. 유명한

5. 제가 이번에 장학생으로 _____.

    ㄱ. 떨어졌어요   ㄴ. 뽑혔어요   ㄷ. 됐어요   ㄹ. 이겼어요

6. 제주도는 돌, 바람, 여자 _____ 유명하다.

    ㄱ. 로   ㄴ. 에   ㄷ. 를   ㄹ. 하고

7. 저희 할아버지는 병으로 _____.

    ㄱ. 돌아보셨어요   ㄴ. 돌아가셨어요   ㄷ. 돌아오셨어요   ㄹ. 돌아 계셨어요

다... 비디오아트는 어떤 예술인지 조사해 보고 같이 이야기해 봅시다.

라... 인터넷에서 백남준의 작품들을 몇 개 찾아보고 여러분의 감상을 이야기해 봅시다.

마... 인터넷에서 김연아의 연기를 찾아보고 여러분의 감상을 이야기해 봅시다.

바... 다음 분야에서 여러분들이 좋아하는 사람들에 대해서 같이 이야기해 봅시다.

    1. 스포츠

    2. 대중 음악

    3. 클래식 음악

    4. 영화, 드라마

    5. 문학

사... 다음은 한국의 역사적 인물들에 대한 영화나 드라마입니다. 이 작품들이나 또는
    한국의 인물을 다룬 작품을 하나 보고 작품 속의 인물에 대해서 이야기해 봅시다.

추 가 읽 기

이순신 장군

한국인들이 가장 존경하는 인물로는 세종 대왕과 함께 이순신 장군이 항상 꼽힌다. 이순신 장군은 조선 시대의 장군으로 일본과의 전쟁인 임진왜란(1592-1598) 때 조선을 지킨 수군의 지휘관이었다.

임진왜란 때 조선의 수군은 정부의 지원을 받지 못해 어려웠지만 이순신 장군은 뛰어난 전술과 지도력으로 모든 전쟁에서 승리했다. 특히 13척의 배로 130여 척의 배를 가진 일본군을 이긴 명량해전은 한국 역사상 최고의 전투로 여겨진다. 임진왜란의 마지막 전투인 노량해전에서 이순신 장군의 함대는 승리했지만 이순신 장군은 일본군의 총에 맞아 전사한다.

그는 훌륭한 군인이었을 뿐만 아니라 인격도 훌륭해서 아직까지 많은 한국인들의 존경을 받고 있다. 이순신 장군이 남긴 말 중에 "죽으려고 하면 살 것이고, 살려고 하면 죽을 것이다!"라는 말은 많은 사람들이 기억하며 그를 본받으려고 노력한다.

장군 general; admiral 꼽히다 to count (as one of the best) 수군 old term for navy
(modern term is 해군) 지휘관 commander 정부 government 지원 support
전술 strategy 지도력 leadership 승리 victory ~척 (counter for ship) 전투 battle
여겨지다 to be considered 해전 sea battle 함대 fleet 총 rifle, gun 전사하다 to die in battle
인격 personality 본받다 to emulate, follow

전래 동화의 인물

다음의 인물들은 한국의 유명한 전래 동화에 나오는 인물들입니다. 여러분 문화에서 유명한 동화 속의 인물들은 누가 있습니까?

홍길동

홍길동은 조선 시대의 유명한 도둑이다. 부자들의 재물을 훔쳐 가난한 사람들을 도와주었다고 한다. 영국의 로빈 후드와 비슷한 인물이다. 소설 "홍길동전"의 인물로도 나온다.

흥부와 놀부

흥부와 놀부는 "흥부전"이라는 소설에 나오는 형제이다. 흥부는 동생으로 아주 착한 사람이고, 형인 놀부는 욕심이 많고 못된 사람이다.

전래 동화 fairy tale 도둑 thief 재물 wealth 가난하다 to be poor 소설 novel 욕심 greed
못되다 to be bad or evil

심청

"심청전"이라는 소설의 여자 주인공이다. 가난한 심청은 눈이 안 보이는 아버지를 위해 자기의 목숨까지 바치는 효녀이다.

성춘향

"춘향전"이라는 소설의 여자 주인공이다. 춘향은 죽을 위기에서도 한 남자를 위해 사랑을 지키는 인물이다.

콩쥐 팥쥐

콩쥐는 신데렐라와 비슷한 인물인데 어렸을 때 어머니가 돌아가시고 새어머니를 맞는다. 새어머니에게는 팥쥐라는 딸이 있는데 새어머니와 팥쥐는 콩쥐를 괴롭힌다.

주인공 main character 목숨 life 바치다 to give, offer 효녀 devoted daughter 위기 crisis
지키다 to keep 괴롭히다 to bully

■■ 번역문 ■■

CONVERSATION: Hangŭl and Korean Language

In the teacher's office

Teacher:	Is studying Korean fun?
Steve:	Yes, but it seems the more I study, the harder it gets.
Teacher:	Hmm…What's the hardest part?
Steve:	Well, Korean pronunciation and grammar is difficult, and honorifics are still hard.
Teacher:	If you keep practicing, soon you will be able to speak Korean well. You're doing a good job in studying Korean, so you don't need to worry.
Steve:	It seems like King Sejong the Great made Korean difficult.
Teacher:	Oh, Sejong the Great created Hangŭl, but he didn't create the Korean language.
Steve:	What? Didn't Sejong the Great create Hangŭl, and that's why Korean people started to use Korean?
Teacher:	Well, a language and its alphabet are not the same thing, you know?
Steve:	Hmm … That's true.
Teacher:	Korean is a language that Korean people have been using for a very long time, it's just that in the past there was no alphabet.
Steve:	Ah …
Teacher:	But Sejong the Great did create an alphabet for the Korean language. That was in 1446, so about 600 years ago.
Steve:	I see. Then how did people write when there was no alphabet?
Teacher:	They wrote using Chinese characters. To put it simply, when speaking people used Korean, but when writing they wrote in Chinese characters what they meant in Korean.
Steve:	Then I guess many people didn't know how to read or write?
Teacher:	Right, so most people at the time couldn't receive an education. Sejong

the Great thought this was unfortunate, and so he made Hangŭl himself.

Steve: Wait, you mean, the king made it himself?

Teacher: Yes, Sejong the Great was intelligent even at a young age, and he stud-
            ied a lot, and that's why they say he was an amazing scholar.

Steve: Wow, he really is a great king!

Teacher: It's not just Hangŭl, people think of Sejong the Great as being the great-
            est king in Korean history because he also had many accomplishments
            in a variety of fields such as science, economy, defense, the arts, and
            culture. He is on the 10,000 won bill, too.

Steve: So that's why at Gwanghwamun there's a statue of Sejong the Great.

Teacher: Now you understand what Hangŭl is clearly, right?

Steve: Yes, and now I know about Sejong the Great as well.

READING 1: Nam June Paik, Video Artist

Nam June Paik is likely the most famous modern artist of Korean descent in the
world. Nam June Paik was the first artist to express himself through using television,
radio, video, and camera to make and develop video art. He was born in 1932 to an
affluent family, and when he was in elementary and middle school he learned how
to play the piano and how to compose music. He went to high school in Hong Kong,
and then he majored in Art History and Music History at the University of Tokyo in
Japan. After graduation, he left to study abroad in Germany where he studied Western architecture, music history, and philosophy, among other subjects.

He became popular through his art performances with many musicians in Germany. During this time, he used television and video to experiment with video art.
Later on, he went to New York in the United States where he became known as a
global video artist. On January 1st, 1984, he attracted worldwide attention for planning a satellite broadcast of "Good Morning, Mr. Orwell", a performance by world
famous artists. His famous works include "Moon is the Oldest TV", "TV-Buddha",
"TV-Cello" and "The More the Better."

Nam June Paik was very active in creating new pieces until the mid-1990s when
he collapsed from a stroke in 1995. In 2006, he passed away at his home in Miami,

United States. Much of Nam June Paik's work is displayed in famous art museums around the world, and many people continue to love his art today.

READING 2: Yuna Kim, Figure Skater

After the 2014 Winter Olympics in Sochi in Russia, the figure skater Yuna Kim retired. However, Yuna Kim is still a global star and a 'national hero'. She has left the ice rink, but Korean people still cherish her dearly. The following is an interview with her.

Reporter: You came in at first-place in a survey asking, "Who is the most charming Korean?" What do you think the reason for that is?

Yuna Kim: Figure skating has not been able to gain much attention in Korea. But I think because I competed with athletes from other countries and won, people have shown more interest in me.

Reporter: How have you spent your time after retiring?

Yuna Kim: When I was a figure skater I was very busy, training five or six times a week. Now that I've retired I don't need to train and I don't need to worry about getting injured, so it's been nice. When I have time in the future I want to travel a lot.

Reporter: And if you look back on your life as a figure skater?

Yuna Kim: There were a lot of painful moments when I was an athlete. I fell and got injured hundreds and thousands of times. I wanted to give up many times. But I think I was able to further mature because of all those painful moments.

At the end, Yuna Kim stated, "I want to be remembered for a long time as the 'Queen of Figure Skating' and the 'Queen on the Ice'."

[Source: JoongAng Daily, an interview with Yuna Kim, the 'Queen on the Ice', 19 months after retirement.]

FURTHER READING: Admiral Yi Sun-sin

Admiral Yi Sun-sin and King Sejong the Great are consistently chosen as the people most respected by Koreans. Yi Sun-sin was an admiral during the Chosŏn era who, as a naval commander, defended Chosŏn during the Japanese invasion of Korea (1592–1598).

At the time of the Japanese invasion of Korea, Admiral Yi Sun-sin was not able to receive proper governmental support, so he faced difficulty. However, with his excellent strategies and leadership skills he won every battle. In particular, the battle of Myŏngnyang, in which 13 ships defeated a Japanese navy made up of about 130 ships, is considered the greatest Korean battle in history. In the last battle of the Japanese invasion of Korea, the battle of Noryang, Yi Sun-sin's fleet was victorious, but Admiral Yi Sun-sin was shot by the Japanese military and he died in battle.

Admiral Yi Sun-sin continues to be respected by Korean people because he was not only an excellent admiral, but also an exceptional person in terms of character. Among the words left behind by Admiral Yi Sun-sin is his statement that "If one intends to die, they will live, and if one intends to live, they will die!" Many people remember these words as they strive to emulate Yi Sun-sin.

CULTURE: Characters from Folk Tales

The following figures are among well-known characters that appear in Korean fairy tales. What are some characters from famous fairy tales in your culture?

- Hong Kildong: Hong Kildong is a famous bandit from the Chosŏn era. He is said to have helped the poor by stealing from the rich. He is a similar character to the English (folklore character) Robin Hood. He appears as a character in the novel Hong Kildong-jŏn.
- Hŭngbu and Nolbu: Hŭngbu and Nolbu are brothers that appear in the novel Hŭngbu-jŏn. Hŭngbu is the younger brother and is a very good man, while Nolbu is a greedy, bad guy.
- Sim Ch'ŏng: Sim Ch'ŏng is the heroine of the novel called Sim Ch'ŏng-jŏn. Sim

Ch'ŏng is a devoted daughter who was willing to give up even her life for her visually impaired father.

- Sŏng Ch'unhyang: Sŏng Ch'unhyang is the heroine of the novel called Ch'unhyang-jŏn. Ch'unhyang is a character who remain steadfast with her love for her man, even when faced with a life-threatening crisis.

- K'ongjwi and Patjwi: Kongjwi is a character, similar to Cinderella, whose mother died when Kongjwi was young. She then comes to live with her stepmother. The stepmother has a daughter named Patjwi, and the stepmother and Patjwi torment Kongjwi.

단어

가난하다	to be poor	발전시키다	to foster, develop
가정	family, home	별세하다	to depart this life
건축	architecture	본받다	to emulate, follow
광화문	Gwanghwamun Gate	부상	injury
괴롭히다	to bully	분야	area, field
국민	(the people of a) nation	선수	player
국방	national defense	성숙해지다	to become mature
귀족 계급	noble class	소설	novel
그리워하다	to miss, long for	수군	old term for navy (modern term is 해군)
글	(a piece of) writing		
기억되다	to be remembered	순간	moment
기자	reporter	쉽게 말하자면	to put it plainly
기획하다	to plan	승리	victory
꼽히다	to count (as one of the best)	실험	experiment
		아픔	pain
뇌졸중	stroke	안타깝다	to be regrettable, pitiful
대단하다	to be incredible	양반	aristocratic class of the Chosŏn Dynasty
도둑	thief		
돌이켜 보다	to look back	업적	achievement
동상	statue	여왕	queen
떠나다	to leave	여유	free time
매력적이다	to be attractive, charming	역사상	historically, in history
		영웅	hero
목숨	life	예술	art
못되다	to be mean or evil	예술가	artist
문법	grammar	욕심	greed
문자	letter, character	위기	crisis
미술사	art history	유복하다	to be rich
바치다	to give, offer	유학	study abroad
발음	pronunciation	은반	ice rink (*lit.* silver plate)

은퇴	retirement	지키다	to guard
은퇴하다	to retire	지폐	bill, paper money
음악사	music history	지원	support
이기다	to win	지휘관	commander
인격	personality	~척	(counter for ship)
인공위성	satellite	철학	philosophy
인물	figure, person	총	rifle, gun
자택	one's own home	총명하다	to be brilliant
작곡	musical composition	포기하다	to give up
작품	work (of art)	표현하다	to express
장군	general; admiral	학자	scholar
재물	wealth	한국계	Korean descent
전래 동화	fairy tale	함대	fleet
전사하다	to die in battle	해전	sea battle
전술	strategy	현대	modern
전투	battle	확실히	clearly
전하다	to tell, convey	활동 무대	one's field of action
정부	government	훌륭하다	to be excellent, splendid
주인공	main character	효녀	devoted daughter
지도력	leadership		

▪▪ Grammar and Usages Index ▪▪

Item	Meaning	GU
대	counter for vehicles, planes, machines, large instruments	GU6.4
대신(에)	instead of	GU2.12
대해(서)	about, in regard to	GU1.1
덕분에	thanks to	GU4.8
~도록	so that ..., to an extent that ... until ...	GU2.4
동	counter for buildings	GU6.4
등	et cetera (etc.), and the like, and so on	GU2.11
따끈하다, 따뜻하다	be fairly hot, adequately hot (to the touch); be warm	GU2.7
~마다	each, every	GU4.12
마리	counter for animals, insects, fish	GU6.4
마음	mind, spirit, feeling, heart, intention	GU3.1
마지막으로	lastly, finally, as the conclusion	GU4.11
매콤하다, 달콤하다	be somewhat spicy hot, to be somewhat sweet	GU2.3
뭐	(oh,) well	GU7.1
및	and, as well as	GU7.7
벌	counter for pair or a set of clothes, plates	GU6.4
~별	(classified) by	GU3.12
별세(하다)	depart this life, pass away	GU7.9
병	bottles, jars	GU6.4
numeral (X) + 분의 + numeral (Y)	numeral (Y) ordinal numeral (X)	GU4.10
분류사	numeral classifiers (or counters)	GU6.4
~뿐(만) 아니라	not only ... (but also ...)	GU1.6
사람, 명, 분 (honorific)	counter for persons, people	GU6.4
생각보다 + adjective/adverb	compared to what I thought	GU4.7
X 생각에(는)	in X's opinion	GU1.2
송이	counter for bunch or cluster of fruits, flowers, snowflake	GU6.4
수~	multiples of (the number)	GU7.11

Item	Meaning	GU
~식	way, style	GU1.9
~ㅆ/았/었어야 하다	one should have done ...	GU4.6
~씩	each, apiece, respectively, per/a, at a time	GU2.5
아니	dear me, why, what, good heavens, well, oh	GU6.2
어떤	certain, some, some kind of	GU1.5
~어/아 두다/놓다	do something for future use/reference	GU1.10
~에 대해서	about, in regard to	GU1.1
~에 따라(서)	depending on ~, following ...	GU4.13
~에 비해(서)	compared to	GU1.3
예를 들어(서)/들면	for example	GU1.8
~와/과(는) 달리/다르게	unlike, differently from	GU6.11
웬만하면, 가능하면	if possible, if you do not mind, if tolerable, if possible	GU4.3
윗사람, 아랫사람	senior, superior vs. junior, subordinate	GU6.9
~(으)ㄴ/는지요?	I am wondering if ...	GU7.10
~(이)나	just; (at least) something or the like; or something like that	GU7.5
~(으)ㄴ 결과	as a result that	GU3.10
~(으)ㄹ까 하다	think of doing, intend to do	GU4.4
~(으)ㄹ 것 없다	there is no need to (do)	GU3.8
~(으)ㄹ 리가 없다	There is no way ... There is no reason why ...	GU3.5
~(으)ㄹ 생각/계획/예정/작정이다	think/plan/intend to (do)	GU4.1
[negation]~(으)ㄹ 수가 없다	be compelled/forced/obliged to; have to; must	GU5.7
~(으)ㄹ 정도로	to the degree or extent to/of ~	GU5.11
~(으)ㄹ지(을/를) 기대하고 있다	to be looking forward to or anticipate that ...	GU5.12
~(으)ㄹ 텐데	I guess/I'm sure that ..., (so, but)	GU6.5
~(으)ㄹ 필요가 있다/없다	It is necessary/unnecessary to	GU1.11
~(으)며	and	GU1.12
~은/는 물론(이고)	not to mention, to say nothing of	GU5.6
~은/는커녕	let alone ~	GU5.5

▪▪ Korean-English Glossary ▪▪

가난하다	to be poor	고개를 숙이다	to bow
가정	family, home	고객	customer
가치관	values	고급	high quality
각 ~마다	for each ~	고급화	to become of a
간단하다	to be simple		higher quality
간단히	briefly	고민	worry, concern
간식	snack	고백	confession
간을 하다	to season with salt or	고소하다	to have rich flavor
	soy sauce	고유	indigenous
간장	soy sauce	고추장	spicy Korean bean paste
간접 화법	indirect quotation	-곳	place
간호사	nurse	공연	performance
갈다	to grind	공통적	common
감독	producer, director	곶감	dried persimmon
감독상	a director award	과장	section chief
감자	potato	관계	relationship
개념	concept	관광지	tourist sites
개인적	personal	관련되다	to be related
개인주의	individualism	관심	interest
건배	cheers	관심을 가지다	to have interests
건축	architecture	광화문	Gwanghwamun Gate
검색하다	to search	괴롭히다	to bully
견과류	nuts	교통사고	traffic accident
결혼 정보 회사	marriage agency	구멍	hole
겹치다	to overlap, double	구별하다	to distinguish
경치	scenery	구분하다	to distinguish
경향	trend	구수하다	to be of rich flavor
경험	experience	구조	structure
계산	calculation	국립공원	national park
계층주의	hierarchism	국물	soup, broth

국민	(people of a) nation	기호	preference
국방	national defense	기회	chance, opportunity
국제	international	기획하다	to plan
국토	country, territory	길거리	street
국화	chrysanthemum	껌	chewing gum
군대	army, military	꼽히다	to count
굴비	partly dried yellow		(as one of the best)
	corvina fish	꿀	honey
굽다	to roast; to bake	끝나다	to be over, done
궁중	royal court	끝내다	to finish (something)
귀족 계급	noble class	끼어들다	to cut in
귀찮다	to be troublesome	나눠먹다	to share food
귤	mandarin orange	나물	wild greens
그러겠다	will do so	나이 들다	to get old
=그렇게 하겠다		나타나다	to appear
그러다가	while so	낙산사	Naksan Temple
그릇	bowl or dish	남	male
그리워하다	to miss, long for	남녀노소	men and women of
그만두다	to stop, quit		all ages
극복하다	to overcome	남편	husband
근데= 그런데	but	남한	South Korea
글	(a piece of) writing	내용	content(s)
기간	period of time	너네들	you (guys)
기대다	to lean on	널리	widely
기대하다	to anticipate	넘다	to be more or over
기록	record	(1990)년대	1990s
기름	oil	-년생	born in year -
기발하다	to be brilliant, novel	노력하다	to try hard
기분	feeling	노출	exposure
기억	memory	녹두	mung bean
기억되다	to be remembered	높낮이	high and low, rise and fall
기자	reporter	놓아 주다	to let go
기준	standard, criteria	뇌졸중	a stroke

누렇다	to be (golden) yellow	독특하다	to be unique
눈에 띄다	to stand out,	돌이켜 보다	to look back
	to attract attention	동감	agreement
느끼다	to feel	동갑	same age
늘어나다	to increase	동남아	Southeast Asia
다양하다	to be various	동상	statue
단백질	protein	동해	the East Sea
단팥	sweet red bean	두각을 나타내다	to distinguish oneself
닭갈비	spicy stir-fried chicken	두어	a couple of
담겨 있다	to be contained	등	etc.
담당하다	to be in charge of	1등급	top-grade
답하다	to answer	등산화	hiking shoes
당면	sweet potato noodle;	등장하다	to appear
	glass noodle	등지	and other places
당연하지!	Of course!	따끈하다	to be warm
당하다	to fall victim for something	따다	to get, obtain
당황하다	to be flustered	따라서	accordingly, therefore
대단하다	to be incredible	따르다	to follow
대리	assistant section chief	따르다¹	to pour
대부분	mostly	따지다²	to argue over
대사	lines or dialogues		(a small matter)
대상	subject	딸애=딸아이	daughter
대신	instead of	떠나다	to leave
대응하다	to react	떨어지다	to fall, drop
대인 관계	interpersonal relations	또한	also
대접	reception, treatment	똑바로	straight, upright
대조적	contrastive	뜻	meaning
대중	public; mass	~로는	as ~
대표적	typical	마약	drugs, narcotics
대하다	to deal with, treat	마음(을) 정리하다	to clear one's mind
더 나아가	furthermore	마음을 끌다	to attract, allure
도둑	thief	마음이 무겁다	to have a heavy heart
도라지	balloon flower root	마음이 식다	to lose interest (in someone)

마찬가지로	similarly	바닥	floor
막걸리	Korean raw rice wine	바람직하다	to be desirable
맡다	to take charge	바위	rock
매달리다	to cling to; to beg	바치다	to give, offer
매력적이다	to be attractive, charming	반도	peninsula
매콤하다	slightly spicy	반드시 = 꼭	for sure; must
맥주	beer	반말	non-honorific language
먹거리	food item	반복	repetition
며느리	daughter-in-law	반죽	dough
명소	famous places	발달하다	to develop
모두	all together	발음	pronunciation
모시다	to accompany;	발전시키다	to foster, develop
	to serve under	방문하다	to visit
모양	shape	방식	way; means
모음	vowel	배	pear
모임	gathering	배경	background
목숨	life	배신	betrayal
목장	ranch	번갈아	alternately; in turn
못되다	to be bad or evil	번지점프	bungee jumping
무지개	rainbow	범위	scope, range
문법	grammar	법적이다	to be legal
문자	letter, character	벚꽃	cherry blossoms
문장	sentence	변하다	to change into
물론이지요	of course	별세하다	to depart this life
뭐(=뭣)	something	보고서	report
미만	less than; below	볶다	to stir-fry
미술사	art history	본받다	to emulate, follow
미역	sea mustard	볼거리	things to see
미주	the Americas	부담	burden
미혼	single; unmarried	부드럽다	to be smooth, soft
민감하다	to be sensitive	부르다	to call
밀가루	flour	부사장	vice president
밀다	to push	부상	injury

부장	division chief	상담자	counselor
부치다	to pan-fry	상당히	considerably
부회장	vice president,	상대방	the other (party)
	vice chairman	상무	managing director
북한	North Korea	상상을 초월하다	to go beyond imagination
분담	share	상업 전략	sales tactic
분석하다	to analyze	상영	showing
분야	area, field	상징하다	to symbolize
4분의 3	three-fourth	상품	products
불과하다	to be mere, just	상황	situation
불꽃(놀이)	fireworks	새해	the New Year
붕어빵	carp-shaped bread	생산되다	to be produced
붙이다	to attach	생선살	fish fillets
비교하다	to compare	생선회	raw fish, sashimi
비용	cost	서생	a young student
비친족어	non-kin terms	서양식	the Western style
빈대떡	mung bean pancake	서해 (=황해)	the Yellow Sea
뿌리다	to sprinkle	섞다	to mix
사모님	one's teacher's or	선배	upperclassman
	senior's wife	선수	player
사용법	usage	선언	announcement
사원	clerk	선지	clotted blood from
사장	company president		slaughtered cows and pigs
사적이다	to be personal	선호	preference
사투리	local dialect	선호하다	to prefer
사회적 지위	social status	설문 조사	survey
살펴보다	to examine	설악산	Seorak Mountain
삼겹살	pork belly meat	섬	island
삼면	three sides	성공하다	to be successful
삼세판	two out of three	성명	full name
삼수	third try for college	성별	sex, gender
	entrance exam	성숙해지다	to become mature
상담	counsel	성장	growth

세대	generation	실제	actual
소설	novel	실험	experiment
소재	subject matter; material	싱글즈	singles
소화	digestion	쓰이다	to be used
속이 든든하다	stomach to be full	씩	each
손을 들다	to raise one's hand(s)	씩씩하다	to be energetic
손을 흔들다	to wave	씹다	to chew
손이 가다	to reach one's hand	아내	wife
	(to eat something)	아드님	one's senior's son
수군	old term for navy	아마	maybe
	(modern term is 해군)	아쉬워하다	to feel the lack of
수출액	amount of export	아쉽다	to feel sorry
순간	moment	아이돌	teen idol
순으로	in order	아이를 낳다	to give birth to a baby
순조롭다	to be smooth	아픔	pain
술자리	drinking party	악수	shaking hands
숫자	number	악화	getting worse
쉽게 말하자면	to put it plainly	(술)안주	snack served with
스푼	spoon		alcoholic beverages
습관	custom; habit	안타깝다	to be sorry; to be pitiful
승리	victory	알감자	baby potatoes
시럽	syrup	알아내다	to find out, figure out
시리얼	breakfast cereal	알아 두다	to keep in mind
시장	market	압도적으로	overwhelmingly
신경을 쓰다	to pay attention to, to care	애인	lover (less formal than 연인)
신기하다	to be surprising, novel	약자	the weak
신선하다	to be fresh	양념	seasoning
신입생	new student	양반	aristocratic class of the
실례	discourtesy		Chosŏn Dynasty
실례하다	to be excused	얕다	to be shallow
실수	mistake	어른	one's elders; adult
실시하다	to conduct	어머	feminine exclamation
실연	breakup; broken heart		"Oh, my!"

어묵	fish cake	예술	art
어서	quickly, please	예술가	artist
어울리다	to go well	예의상	out of courtesy
억양	intonation	예의에 어긋나다	to go against manners
언어 예절	language etiquette	예전	the past
얻다	to gain	예절	etiquette
얼음	ice	오래가다	to last long
업적	achievement	오래되다	to have been old
~에 대해서	about	오징어	squid
~에 비해서	compare to ~	옥수수	corn
여겨지다	to be considered	~와/과 달리	unlike ~
여러 가지	various, many	완성	completion
여왕	queen	완성하다	to complete
여유	free (time)	외모	appearance
역사상	historically, in history	~ 외에	other than ~
역할을 하다	to play a role	요리	cooked dish
연말	end of the year	욕심	greed
연수	(educational) training	운명	fate; destiny
연애	date	운이 좋다	to be lucky
연예인	entertainer	운전 면허	driver's license
연유	condensed milk	원래	originally
연인	one's lover; two lovers	월급	salary
연중	year-round	웬만하면	if possible
연휴	long weekend	위기	crisis
열풍	hot wind or fever	위치하다	to be located
영문학과	English Literature Department	윗사람	someone of older or higher status
영양가	nutrition	유능하다	to be competent
영어권	English-speaking regions	유복하다	to be affluent
영웅	hero	유제품	dairy products
영향	influence	유지하다	to maintain
영화제	film festival	유학	study abroad
예를 들어	for example	유행을 타다	to go along the trend

–으니	formal form of –으니까	인종	race, ethnic group
은반	ice rink (*lit.* silver plate)	인턴 사원	internship clerk
은퇴하다	to retire	인형 조형물	iconic doll sculptures
음란	obscene	일 인분	a serving for one
음악사	history of music	일시적	temporary, momentary
응답자	respondent	입학하다	to enter a school
의견	opinion	잊다	to forget
의미	meaning	잊혀지다	to be forgotten
의사소통	communication	자기	oneself
의외로	unexpectedly	자녀	children, sons and
이 밖에	besides		daughters
이기다	to win	자라다	to grow (up), be raised
이리 = 이쪽으로	this way	자세	attitude
이모	aunt (mom's sister)	자연스럽게	naturally
이사	a director (of board of	자음	consonant
	directors)	자택	one's own home
이상	over; and more than	작곡	musical composition
이어	following	작품	work (of art)
이외	besides, except	잔치국수	a party noodle dish
이용	use	잠시 후	after a while
이유	reason	장군	general; admiral
이제	now	재료	ingredients
익히다¹	to master	재물	wealth
익히다²	to cook	재미를 더하다	to add fun
인간 관계	human relations	재배되다	to be cultivated
인격	personality	재수하다	to study for the second
인공위성	satellite		try to enter a college
인기가 높다	to be popular	적극적	to be active
인물	figure, person	적당히	moderately
인사 드리다	to greet a senior	적절하게	appropriately, properly
인삼	*insam* (ginseng)	적절하다	to be appropriate
인생	one's life	전래 동화	fairy tale
인연	affinity; fate	전무	executive director

전사하다	to die in battle	주간	weekly
전술	strategy	주로	mostly, mainly
전시하다	to display or exhibit	주위	surrounding
전자공학	electrical engineering	주의하다	to be cautious, careful
전체	the whole	주인공	main character
전통	tradition	주제곡	theme song
전투	battle	줄이다	to reduce
전하다	to tell, convey	중독되다	to become addicted
전혀	(not) at all	중독성	addiction
절	Buddhist temple	중동	the Middle East
절대	absolute	중반	the middle phase
젊다	to be young, youthful	중심	center
젊은이	young people	즐기다	to enjoy
-점	thing, point	증거	proof, evidence
점원	clerk	지도력	leadership
접속	access	지리	geography
젓갈	salted seafood	지방	regions except Seoul and
정답	right answer		its vicinity
정당	political party	지역별	by locations
정보	information	지원	support
정부	government	지지하다	to support
조리법	cooking method	지칭어	reference terms
조사되다	to be investigated	지칭하다	to call, refer to
조화	harmony	지키다	to guard
조회 수	number of views or searches	지폐	bill, paper money
존대법	honorifics	지형	geographical features
존댓말	honorific language	지휘관	commander
존중하다	to respect	직원	clerk, employee
좀	just	직함	job title
종교	religion	진심으로	truly
종류	type	진행되다	to progress
주 ~회	~ times a week	질서	social order
주가	stock price	집계되다	to be summed up

집단주의	collectivism
집사람	my wife
집중하다	to concentrate
짓다	to form
짝수	even number
쫄깃쫄깃하다	to be chewy
찌다	to steam
차갑다	one's attitude to be cold
차이	difference
차이점	difference
차장	assistant division chief
차지하다	to be ranked
찹쌀	glutinous rice, sticky rice
창자	intestines
채우다	to fill
처럼	like, as if
처음엔=처음에는	at first
척	counter for boats and ships
철분	iron
철판 틀	metal mold
철학	philosophy
청취자	radio listener
체중	body weight
총	rifle, gun
총명하다	to be brilliant
총무	manager
촬영지	filming site
촬영하다	to film
최고	the best
최근	recent(ly)
최근에	lately
추억	recollection, reminiscence
출출하다	to be a little hungry

취기	the effects of alcohol
친밀함	intimacy
친족어	kinship terms
친척	relative
친하다	to be close
칭찬	compliment
캔	can
커플링	matching rings between lovers
켤레	a pair (of hand and foot wear)
크기	size
타인	other people
탁하다	to be murky
태극기 휘날리며	the movie "Taegukgi, Brotherhood of War" (lit. Fluttering the Korean flag)
터지다	to burst
토론	discussion, debate
토핑	topping
통닭	roasted whole-chicken
통장	bankbook, bank account
통하다	to go through
투표권	right to vote
튀기다	to deep-fry
특산물	regional products
특이하다	to be unique
특정	specific
특징	characteristics
특히	especially
팥빙수	shaved ice with sweet red beans

퍼져 나가다	to spread out	해외	overseas
평균	average	해전	sea battle
평등주의	egalitarianism	행동하다	to behave
포기하다	to give up	헤어지다	to break up
포장마차	covered street cart bar	현대	modern
포함하다	to include	현상	phenomenon
표시하다	to mark, indicate	호두	walnut
표준어	standard language	호칭어	address terms
표현	expression	호칭하다	to call, address
표현하다	to express	혹시	by any chance
풀빵	bread with filling	홀수	odd number
	made stove-top	홍련암	Hongnyeonam
피서지	summer resort		(Small Temple)
학번	the year when one enters	홍보	PR
	a college	확실히	clearly
학업	study	환영회	welcoming party
학자	scholar	환자	patient
한국전쟁	Korean War	활동 무대	one's field of action
한국계	Korean descent	회장	chairman of a corporation
한국방송광고	Korea Broadcast	회장	president of a club
진흥공사	Advertising Corporation	횟수	number of times
한옥마을	village of Korean houses	효과	effect
한우	Korean beef	효녀	devoted daughter
한입	a single bite	후유증	aftereffect
함대	fleet	훈련	training
합치다	to combine	훌륭하다	to be excellent, splendid
항구	harbor, port	휴게실	lounge
해	year	흔들리다	to be shaken
해돋이	sunrise	흔적	trace
해수욕장	beach	흔히	common
해안	coast		

◼◼ English-Korean Glossary ◼◼

English	Korean
1990s	1990년대
about	~에 대해서
absolute	절대
access	접속
accordingly, therefore	따라서
achievement	업적
actual	실제
addiction	중독성
address terms	호칭어
affinity; fate	인연
after a while	잠시 후
aftereffect	후유증
agreement	동감
all together	모두
also	또한
alternately; in turn	번갈아
Americas	미주
amount of export	수출액
and other places	등지
announcement	선언
appearance	외모
appropriately, properly	적절하게
architecture	건축
area, field	분야
aristocratic class of the Chosŏn Dynasty	양반
army, military	군대
art	예술
art history	미술사
artist	예술가
as ~	~로는
assistant division chief	차장
assistant section chief	대리
at first	처음엔 =처음에는
attitude	자세
aunt (mom's sister)	이모
average	평균
baby potatoes	알감자
background	배경
balloon flower root	도라지
bankbook, bank account	통장
battle	전투
beach	해수욕장
beer	맥주
besides	이 밖에
besides, except	이외
best	최고
best of three	삼세판
betrayal	배신
bill, paper money	지폐
body weight	체중
born in year -	-년생
bowl or dish	그릇
bread with filling made stove-top	풀빵
breakfast cereal	시리얼
breakup; broken heart	실연
briefly	간단히
Buddhist temple	절
bungee jumping	번지점프

burden	부담	confession	고백
but	근데= 그런데	considerably	상당히
by any chance	혹시	consonant	자음
by locations	지역별	contrastive	대조적
calculation	계산	cooked dish	요리
can	캔	cooking method	조리법
carp-shaped bread	붕어빵	corn	옥수수
center	중심	cost	비용
chairman of a corporation	회장	content(s)	내용
chance	기회	counsel	상담
characteristics	특징	counselor	상담자
cherry blossoms	벚꽃	counter for ship	척
chewing gum	껌	country, territory	국토
children	자녀	a couple of	두어
chrysanthemum	국화	covered street cart bar	포장마차
clearly	확실히	crisis	위기
clerk (of a company)	사원	custom; habit	습관
clerk (of a store)	점원	customer	고객
employee	직원	dairy products	유제품
clotted blood from	선지	date	연애
slaughtered cows and pigs		daughter	딸애
coast	해안	daughter-in-law	며느리
collectivism	집단주의	deputy chairman	부회장
commander	지휘관	deputy section chief	대리
common	공통적	devoted daughter	효녀
commonly	흔히	difference	차이
communication	의사소통	difference	차이점
company president	사장	digestion	소화
compare to ...	~에 비해서	director (of board of directors)	이사
completion	완성	director award	감독상
compliment	칭찬	discourtesy	실례
concept	개념	discussion, debate	토론
condensed milk	연유	division chief	부장

dough	반죽	fireworks	불꽃(놀이)
dried persimmon	곶감	first grade, rate	1등급
drinking party	술자리	fish cake	어묵
driver's license	운전 면허	fish fillets	생선살
drugs, narcotics	마약	fleet	함대
each	씩	floor	바닥
East Sea	동해	flour	밀가루
effect	효과	following	이어
effects of alcohol	취기	food item	먹거리
egalitarianism	평등주의	for each ~	각 ~마다
electrical engineering	전자공학	for example	예를 들어
end of the year	연말	formal form of -으니까	-으니
English Department	영문학과	free (time)	여유
English-speaking regions	영어권	full name	성명
entertainer	연예인	furthermore	더 나아가
especially	특히	gathering	모임
etc.	등	general; admiral	장군
etiquette	예절	generation	세대
even number	짝수	geographical features	지형
executive director	전무	geography	지리
experience	경험	getting worse	악화
experiment	실험	glutinous rice, sticky rice	찹쌀
exposure	노출	grammar	문법
expression	표현	greed	욕심
fairy tale	전래 동화	growth	성장
family, home	가정	Gwanghwamun Gate	광화문
famous places	명소	harbor, port	항구
fate; destiny	운명	harmony	조화
feeling	기분	wild greens	나물
feminine exclamation "Oh, my!"	어머	hero	영웅
figure, person	인물	hierarchism	계층주의
film festival	영화제	high and low, rise and fall	높낮이
filming site	촬영지	high quality	고급

hiking shoes	등산화	iron	철분
historically, in history	역사상	island	섬
history of music	음악사	just some things	뭐(=뭣) 좀
hole	구멍	kinship terms	친족어
honey	꿀	Korea Broadcast	한국방송광고
Hongnyeonam (Small Temple)	홍련암	Advertising Corporation	진흥공사
honorific form of 아들 or son	아드님	Korean beef	한우
honorific language	존댓말	Korean descent	한국계
honorifics	존대법	Korean War	한국전쟁
hot wind or fever	열풍	language etiquette	언어 예절
human relations	인간 관계	lately	최근에
husband	남편	leadership	지도력
ice	얼음	less than; below	미만
ice rink (*lit.* silver plate)	은반	letter, character	문자
iconic doll sculptures	인형 조형물	life	목숨
if possible	웬만하면	like, as if	처럼
in order	순으로	lines or dialogues	대사
indigenous	고유	local speech	사투리
indirect quotation	간접 화법	long weekend	연휴
individualism	개인주의	lounge	휴게실
influence	영향	lover (less formal than 연인)	애인
information	정보	main character	주인공
ingredients	재료	male	남
injury	부상	managing director	상무
insam (ginseng)	인삼	mandarin orange	귤
instead of	대신	market	시장
interest	관심	marriage agency	결혼 정보 회사
international	국제	matching rings between lovers	커플링
internship clerk	인턴 사원	maybe	아마
interpersonal relations	대인 관계	meaning	뜻
intestines	창자	meaning	의미
intimacy	친밀함	memory	기억
intonation	억양	men and women of all ages	남녀노소

metal mold	철판 틀	of course	물론이지요
Middle East	중동	Of course!	당연하지!
middle phase	중반	oil	기름
mistake	실수	old term for navy	수군
moderately	적당히	(modern term is 해군)	
modern	현대	one's attitude to be cold	차갑다
mostly	대부분	one's elders; adult	어른
mostly, mainly	주로	one's field of action	활동 무대
mung bean	녹두	one's own home	자택
mung bean pancake	빈대떡	one's teacher's or senior's wife	사모님
musical composition	작곡	one's life	인생
must	반드시 = 꼭	one's lover; two lovers	연인
Naksan Temple	낙산사	oneself	자기
national defense	국방	opinion	의견
national park	국립공원	opportunity	기회
naturally	자연스럽게	originally	원래
new student	신입생	other (party)	상대방
New Year	새해	other people	타인
noble class	귀족 계급	other than ~	~ 외에
non-honorific language	반말	out of courtesy	예의상
non-kin terms	비친족어	over; and more than	이상
North Korea	북한	overseas	해외
not at all	전혀	overwhelmingly	압도적으로
novel	소설	pain	아픔
now	이제	pair (of hand and foot wear)	켤레
number	숫자	partly dried yellow corvina fish	굴비
number of times	횟수	party noodle dish	잔치국수
number of views or searches	조회 수	past	예전
nurse	간호사	patient	환자
nutrition	영양가	pear	배
nuts	견과류	peninsula	반도
obscene	음란	people of a nation	국민
odd number	홀수	performance	공연

period of time	기간	reference terms	지칭어
personal	개인적	regional products	특산물
personality	인격	regions except Seoul	지방
phenomenon	현상	and its vicinity	
philosophy	철학	relationship	관계
piece of writing	글	relative	친척
place	-곳	religion	종교
player	선수	repetition	반복
political party	정당	report	보고서
pork belly meat	삼겹살	reporter	기자
potato	감자	respondent	응답자
PR	홍보	rifle, gun	총
preference	선호	right answer	정답
preference for, taste	기호	right to vote	투표권
president of a club	회장	roasted whole-chicken	통닭
producer, director	감독	rock	바위
products	상품	royal court	궁중
pronunciation	발음	salary	월급
proof, evidence	증거	sales tactic	상업 전략
protein	단백질	salted seafood	젓갈
public; mass	대중	same age	동갑
queen	여왕	satellite	인공위성
quickly, please	어서	scenery	경치
race, ethnic group	인종	scholar	학자
radio listener	청취자	scope, range	범위
rainbow	무지개	sea battle	해전
ranch	목장	sea mustard	미역
raw fish, sashimi	생선회	seasoning	양념
reason	이유	section chief	과장
recent(ly)	최근	sentence	문장
reception, treatment	대접	Seorak Mountain	설악산
recollection, reminiscence	추억	serving for one	일 인분
record	기록	sex, gender	성별

shaking hands	악수	straight, upright	똑바로
shape	모양	strategy	전술
share	분담	street	길거리
shaved ice with sweet red beans	팥빙수	stroke	뇌졸중
showing	상영	structure	구조
similarly	마찬가지로	study	학업
single bite	한입	study abroad	유학
single; unmarried	미혼	subject	대상
singles	싱글즈	subject matter; material	소재
situation	상황	summer resort	피서지
size	크기	sunrise	해돋이
slightly spicy	매콤하다	surrounding	주위
snack	간식	survey	설문 조사
snack served with alcoholic beverages	(술)안주	sweet potato noodle; glass noodle	당면
social order	질서	sweet red bean	단팥
social status	사회적 지위	syrup	시럽
someone of older or higher status	윗사람	"Taegukgi, Brotherhood of War" (*lit.* Fluttering the Korean Flag), the movie	태극기 휘날리며
soup, broth	국물		
South Korea	남한	teen idol	아이돌
Southeast Asia	동남아	temporary, momentary	일시적
soy sauce	간장	theme song	주제곡
specific	특정	thief	도둑
spicy Korean bean paste	고추장	thing, point	-점
spicy stir-fried chicken	닭갈비	things to see	볼거리
spoon	스푼	third try for college entrance exam	삼수
squid	오징어		
standard, criteria	기준	this way	이리 = 이쪽으로
standard language	표준어	three sides	삼면
statue	동상	three-fourths	4분의 3
stock price	주가	times a week	주~회
stomach to be full	속이 든든하다	to accompany, to serve under	모시다

to add fun	재미를 더하다	to be investigated	조사되다
to analyze	분석하다	to be legal	법적이다
to answer	답하다	to be located	위치하다
to anticipate	기대하다	to be lucky	운이 좋다
to appear	나타나다	to be mere, just	불과하다
to argue over (a small matter)	따지다	to be more or over	넘다
to attach	붙이다	to be murky	탁하다
to attract, allure	마음을 끌다	to be of rich flavor	구수하다
to be (golden) yellow	누렇다	to be over, done	끝나다
to be a little hungry	출출하다	to be personal	사적이다
to be active	적극적	to be poor	가난하다
to be affluent	유복하다	to be popular	인기가 높다
to be appropriate	적절하다	to be produced	생산되다
to be attractive, charming	매력적이다	to be ranked	차지하다
to be bad or evil	못되다	to be related	관련되다
to be brilliant	총명하다	to be remembered	기억되다
to be brilliant, novel	기발하다	to be sensitive	민감하다
to be cautious, careful	주의하다	to be shaken	흔들리다
to be chewy	쫄깃쫄깃하다	to be shallow	얕다
to be close	친하다	to be simple	간단하다
to be competent	유능하다	to be smooth	순조롭다
to be considered	여겨지다	to be smooth, soft	부드럽다
to be contained	담겨있다	to be sorry; to be pitiful	안타깝다
to be cultivated	재배되다	to be successful	성공하다
to be desirable	바람직하다	to be summed up	집계되다
to be energetic	씩씩하다	to be surprising, novel	신기하다
to be excellent, splendid	훌륭하다	to be troublesome	귀찮다
to be excused	실례하다	to be unique	특이하다
to be flustered	당황하다	to be unique	독특하다
to be forgotten	잊혀지다	to be used	쓰이다
to be fresh	신선하다	to be various	다양하다
to be in charge of	담당하다	to be warm	따끈하다
to be incredible	대단하다	to be young, youthful	젊다

to become addicted	중독되다	to enjoy	즐기다
to become mature	성숙해지다	to enter a school	입학하다
to become of a higher quality	고급화	to examine	살펴보다
to behave	행동하다	to express	표현하다
to bow	고개를 숙이다	to fall, drop	떨어지다
to break up	헤어지다	to fall victim for something	당하다
to bully	괴롭히다	to feel	느끼다
to burst	터지다	to feel sorry	아쉽다
to call	부르다	to feel the lack of	아쉬워하다
to call, address	호칭하다	to fill	채우다
to call, refer to	지칭하다	to film	촬영하다
to change into	변하다	to find out, figure out	알아내다
to chew	씹다	to finish (something)	끝내다
to clear one's mind	마음(을) 정리하다	to follow	따르다
to cling to; to beg	매달리다	to forget	잊다
to combine	합치다	to form	짓다
to compare	비교하다	to foster, develop	발전시키다
to complete	완성하다	to gain	얻다
to concentrate	집중하다	to get, obtain	따다
to conduct	실시하다	to get old	나이 들다
to cook	익히다	to give, offer	바치다
to count (as one of the best)	꼽히다	to give birth to a baby	아이를 낳다
to cut in	끼어들다	to give up	포기하다
to deal, treat	대하다	to go against manners	예의에 어긋나다
to deep-fry	튀기다	to go along the trend	유행을 타다
to depart this life	별세하다	to go beyond imagination	상상을 초월하다
to develop	발달하다	to go through	통하다
to die in battle	전사하다	to go well	어울리다
to display or exhibit	전시하다	to greet a senior	인사 드리다
to distinguish	구별하다	to grind	갈다
to distinguish, classify	구분하다	to grow (up), be raised	자라다
to distinguish oneself	두각을 나타내다	to guard	지키다
to emulate, follow	본받다	to have a heavy heart	마음이 무겁다

to have been old	오래되다	to respect	존중하다
to have interests	관심을 가지다	to retire	은퇴하다
to have rich flavor	고소하다	to roast; to bake	굽다
to include	포함하다	to search	검색하다
to increase	늘어나다	to season with salt or soy sauce	간을 하다
to keep in mind	알아 두다	to share food	나눠 먹다
to last long	오래가다	to spread out	퍼져 나가다
to lean on	기대다	to sprinkle	뿌리다
to leave	떠나다	to stand out, to attract attention	눈에 띄다
to let go	놓아 주다	to steam	찌다
to look back	돌이켜 보다	to stir-fry	볶다
to lose interest (in someone)	마음이 식다	to stop, quit	그만두다
to maintain	유지하다	to study for the second try to	재수하다
to mark, indicate	표시하다	enter a college	
to master	익히다	to support	지지하다
to miss, long for	그리워하다	to symbolize	상징하다
to mix	섞다	to take charge	맡다
to overcome	극복하다	to tell, convey	전하다
to overlap, double	겹치다	to try hard	노력하다
to pan-fry	부치다	to visit	방문하다
to pay attention to, to care	신경을 쓰다	to wave	손을 흔들다
to plan	기획하다	to win	이기다
to play a role	역할을 하다	topping	토핑
to pour	따르다	tourist sites	관광지
to prefer	선호하다	trace	흔적
to progress	진행되다	tradition	전통
to push	밀다	traditional Korean rice wine	막걸리
to put it plainly	쉽게 말하자면	traffic accident	교통사고
to raise one's hand(s)	손을 들다	training	연수
to reach one's hand	손이 가다	training	훈련
(to eat something)		trend	경향
to react	대응하다	type	종류
to reduce	줄이다	typical	대표적

unexpectedly	의외로	Western style	서양식
unlike ~	~와/과 달리	while so	그러다가
upper classmate	선배	whole	전체
usage	사용법	widely	널리
use	이용	wife	아내
values	가치관	my wife	집사람
various, many	여러 가지	will do so	그러겠다
vice president	부사장		=그렇게 하겠다
victory	승리	work (of art)	작품
village of Korean houses	한옥마을	worry, concern	고민
vowel	모음	year	해
walnut	호두	year when one enters a college	학번
way; means	방식	year-round	연중
weak	약자	Yellow Sea	서해 (=황해)
wealth	재물	you (guys)	너네들
weekly	주간	young people	젊은이
welcoming party	환영회	a young student	서생

CREDITS

All illustrations, except p. 208: Han Sejin, Circus Image Works Co., Ltd.

Pp. 49–51: "The World of Popular Street Food", Kwŏn Sŭng-jun and Km Hyŏng-wŏn, *JoongAng Ilbo*, 2011

Pp. 49–51: *Pungŏppang-edo Chokpo-ka Iitta*, Yun Dŏk-no, Jeonju: Ch'ŏngbori, 2011

P. 60: "'Ch'imaek' and Electronics Stock Prices that Rise during the Olympics . . . Rio de Janeiro, Too?", *Chosun Biz*, 2016

P. 60: "Fifty Years of Ch'ik'o-nomi' . . . The First Appearance of Myeong-dong Nutrition Center's Rotisserie Chicken in 1960s", *The Dong-A Ilbo*, 2013

P. 60: "'Samgyŏpsal', Seoul's Best Food Selected by Foreigners", *Asia Economy Daily*, 2011

Pp. 84–85: "When Is the Best Time to Date for Single Men and Women in Their 20s to 30s? Men Said Evenings, and Women Said . . . ", *JOINS*, 2011

P. 95: "How Long Is There to Be No-Dating after a Break-Up, as Decided by Men of Affection? How Long Is It in Reality? For How Long Should They Not Start a New Relationship after Breaking-Up?", *EDAILY*, 2011

P. 107: Blank Maps of the Republic of Korea, National Geographic Information Institute of Ministry of Land, Infrastructure and Transport

Pp. 123, 132: http://kangzip.tistory.com/m/446, Yet Another Knowledge, Korea's Blank Maps of Districts, Counties, and Cities, Kang P'il

Pp. 158–160: "*Hallyu*, Began 15 Years Ago in China . . . beyond Asia to the World", *Radio Free Asia*

Pp. 158–160: "K-Pop", *Doosan Encyclopedia*

Pp. 171–173: Recommended Attractions for *Hallyu*, Seoul Metropolitan Government Seoul Tourism Organization

P. 208: *Power up Korean Vocabulary*, Yoon Sang-Seok, Ko Insung, Son Jung Min, Seoul: Korea University Press, 2015

P. 232: Nam June Paik, Chongro Cross, 1991. San Francisco Museum of Modern Art, Phyllis C. Wattis Fund for Major Accessions © Estate of Nam June Paik, Photograph by Katherine Du Tiel

Pp. 233–234: "An Interview with the 'Queen of the Ice,' 19 Months of Retirement, 'Passion and Tenacity Are Korea's Appeal, As for Me, I Showcased Them through Figure Skating'", *JoongAng Ilbo*